THE PHILADELPHIA BIG 5

Great Moments in Philadelphia's Storied College Basketball History

Donald Hunt

SAGAMORE PUBLISHING
Champaign, IL 61820

Book design, editor: Susan McKinney
Cover design: Michelle R. Dressen
Proofreader: Phyllis L. Bannon

ISBN:1-57167-070-x
Library of Congress Catalog Card Number:96-71296

Sagamore Publishing
804 N. Neil Suite 100
Champaign, IL 61824-0647
www.sagamorepub.com

Printed in the United States.

This book is dedicated to my mother and father.
It is also dedicated to all those who can do and will do,
but just need an opportunity to succeed.

CONTENTS

ACKNOWLEDGMENTS

Writing this book was a real labor of love for me. I've always enjoyed Big 5 basketball. But I couldn't have accomplished this project without the help of many sharp basketball minds in the Philadelphia area.

First, I would like to thank all the fine sports information people in the Big 5, such as Al Shrier and Scott Cathcart (Temple), Ken Krsolovic and Larry Dougherty (St. Joseph's), Bob Vetrone (La Salle), Gail Stasulli Zachary and Shaun May (Pennsylvania) and Karen Frascona (Villanova) and Gary Emig, former Temple sports information director, now at Ohio State, for bio information on coaches, teams and players.

Next, I would like to thank all the Big 5 athletic directors Bob Mullen (La Salle), Steve Bilsky (Pennsylvania), Don DiJulia (St. Joseph's), Dave O'Brien (Temple) and Gene DeFilippo (Villanova) for all their support in this project.

I would like to thank Herm Rogul, former *Bulletin* sports columnist, Barnett Wright, managing editor of *The Philadelphia Tribune*, Bob Vetrone, Jr., assistant sports information director at La Salle, Dick Jerardi, sports writer of *The Philadelphia Daily News*, and Bret Hoover, of Hoover Graphics, for providing editing, articles, interesting vignettes and statistics.

Finally, I would like to thank my wife, Pat and son, Little Don, who demonstrated great patience and understanding during the time I was writing the book.

I would like to especially thank Dan Baker, who recently retired after 15 years as Executive Director of the Big 5 for all his help with the book. Dan provided me with a great deal of photos and information on the Philadelphia Big 5.

The Big 5 has always been very special to him as well as many other fans in the Philadelphia area. During his career with the Big 5, he was instrumental in putting together the Hall of Fame luncheons, Big 5 Meet the Media night (a preseason dinner for the sportswriters, broadcasters and local teams) radio and television broadcasts and many other activities. He also negotiated the Big 5 contracts that allowed the five schools to continue to play each other each year.

Although Dan won't be handling the administrative functions on a daily basis, he will remain very close to the Big 5 by working as a color analyst on the radio broadcasts for all the games. Paul Rubincam, former athletic director at the University of Pennsylvania, has agreed to succeed Dan as executive director of the Big 5.

FOREWORD

Extremely fortunate is how anyone who has been associated with the Big 5 surely feels. Fans, students, players, referees, coaches, opponents, opposing coaches and the media have recognized for the past 40 years that something very special existed within the Philadelphia basketball community. The Big 5 touched the hearts of all in a unique way. So often we hear what is wrong in our world; the Philadelphia Big 5 is what is right and has been right about intercollegiate athletics and college basketball.

Of course, the Philadelphia Big 5 is almost synonymous with the Palestra, the hallowed pit where so many great players and coaches entertained the avid spectators who knew they were privileged to be witnessing something to be cherished. In an era when life in our country has become increasingly complicated, the Palestra and the Philadelphia Big 5 remain a constant source of the purity of competition and a simplicity that causes one to reflect with fondness, to savor the oh-so-many glorious times.

The storied names and Hall of Fame careers that took shape here; the anonymous managers, equipment men, mascots and statisticians who dutifully performed and felt honored to do so; the security personnel in dark business suits, wearing black leather belts and black hats later traded for jackets or blazers; the notable fans and characters, perhaps best represented by Yo Yo, the unofficial number one fan; the extraordinary media coverage and personalities who professed their objectivity but were sucked into the partisan vacuum labeled Palestra and privately rooted for the local combatants; the cheerleaders, the rollouts, the drum, Cavanaugh's pre or post game— all just a bit of the flavor of Philadelphia basketball Big 5 style.

Chuck Daly once told me that as he and then assistant, Rollie Massimino were on their way from their locker to the bench for their first ever Big 5 game as Penn coaches, they paused under the basket. The teams were finishing their warm-ups, the bands were blaring fight songs, cheerleaders jumping, mascots dueling and the fans already in a frenzy. Daly turned to Massimino and said, "This is what it is supposed to be like." Penn lost that night to Temple, but Daly, Massimino, the players, fans and anyone who saw that Big 5 contest were winners long term, for being part of such tradition.

The Philadelphia Big 5 has added value to the lives of those that it has touched and we will be forever grateful for the experience. Not all have been recognized or honored for their achievements at the Big 5 and beyond, but all that have been exposed to it share a common bond, a feeling of family, of a special place and time stored in the fondest parts of hearts and memory.

John Nash
Former Executive Director of the Big 5
General Manager of the New Jersey Nets

PREFACE

I grew up in Darby, Pennsylvania, where there were Big 5 fans all over town. Darby has produced a lot of great players over the years. Few attended Big 5 schools, but we had some representation in the Philadelphia college basketball scene.

Pete Coleman, who led Darby High School to back-to-back PIAA state championships in 1962 and 1963, played a short time at Villanova. My freshman basketball coach at Darby-Colwyn, Gary Kasmer, played four years at Temple.

However, the most prominent player from Darby to play in the Big 5 was Eddie Mast. Mast was the starting center on Temple's 1969 NIT championship team coached by Harry Litwack. Mast wasn't a great high school player; in fact, there were a lot of players in Darby who were better than him. Mast only played one year of high school basketball. But he was 6-10 and did improve his game by playing with Hal Booker, Sonny Realer, Pete Coleman, Walt Carey and many other standouts from Darby.

When the Owls won the NIT in 1969, I was in ninth grade at Darby-Colwyn Junior High School. During that time, I didn't know that Mast was playing for Temple, until one day when I saw the Owls playing on television.

Mast and Kasmer weren't the only players from Darby to wear the Cherry and White for the Owls. Kevin Clifton played four years for John Chaney, who tried to recruit him for Cheyney State. Clifton, who didn't receive a lot of playing time during his career, made the big pass to Terence Stansbury in the NCAA tournament in 1984 against St. John's. Stansbury took Clifton's pass about 40 feet away from the basket and hit a last-second shot to beat St. John's for the Owls' first NCAA win since 1958.

Alonzo Lewis is the other notable basketball player from Darby High School to play in the Big 5. Lewis was an All-Big 5 standout with La Salle.

What I remember the most was watching the Big 5 games on WPHL-TV Channel 17. The announcers were Al Meltzer, Charlie Swift, Richie Ashburn, Harry Kalas and Bob Vetrone. My brother Jim and I used to watch the games on television at home. We would also go over to my uncle's (Reynal Tripp) house to watch Big 5 Hall of Famers Howard Porter, Ken Durrett, Fran O'Hanlon, John Baum, Mike Bantom, Bernie Williams, Roland Taylor, Johnny Jones and many others. His favorite at that time was La Salle. I enjoyed watching La Salle, but my favorite team was Temple.

I remember watching Durrett score 45 points against Jim McDaniels, an All-American and first-round draft pick from Western Kentucky. There were a number of great college players who visited the Palestra such as Calvin Murphy, Bill Bradley, Austin Carr, Spencer Haywood, Patrick Ewing, Kenny Smith, Johnny Dawkins, Brian Taylor and Mark Aguirre.

I enjoyed watching the Big 5 matchups at the Palestra. But whenever a nationally ranked team played a Big 5 school that was always something special. The Big 5 schools have developed a reputation for knocking off the top teams in college basketball.

I was among the many fans who watched these outstanding games at the Palestra during the '70s. In the '80s and '90s, I had a chance to cover a lot of the Big 5 games as a sportswriter for the Philadelphia Tribune. I also had an opportunity to chronicle the great players in *The Sporting News*, *Basketball Weekly*, *USA Today*, *Street and Smith's College Basketball Yearbook* and *Eastern Basketball*.

The only thing different about the Big 5 today as opposed to yesterday is most of the games are not played at the Palestra and the schools don't play a full round-robin schedule. Other than that, the great players, great moments and the great games are still here.

Donald Hunt

INTRODUCTION

My greatest professional break was to jump from coaching basketball at Mt. Pleasant, a small high school situated on the fringe of Wilmington, Delaware, to become the head man at St. Joseph's College (now University) in 1955, the same year the Big 5 started.

It happened because of a chance summer meeting at a Phillies baseball game with the Reverend Joseph M. Geib, SJ, then moderator of athletics at St. Joseph's. Father Geib knew me as a former player at St. Joseph's, and that I was coaching high school ball in the area. We talked about the current Hawks team; and then he asked about my teams—which happened to be doing pretty well—and about my future plans—which hopefully were to coach at the college level. Two days later, he called to ask if I would be interested in coaching the Hawks. I almost jumped through the phone.

I inherited a talented group of upper classmen—Mike Fallon, Bill Lynch, Kurt Engelbert, Al Juliana, Dan Dougherty, Ray Radziszewski, Jack McKinney and Jimmy Purcell—that had soaked up valuable experience under my predecessor, John McMenamin. It was a hungry team, ready to win. And win we did — the Big 5 title, participation in St. Joseph's first post-season tournament (a third-place finish in the NIT), and a 23-6 record.

It was an incredible, storybook kind of year, but the thing I remember most was the Big 5 championship game with Temple. The Owls' wonder team of Guy Rodgers, Hal Lear, Jay Norman, Harold "Hotsy" Reinfeld, and Tink Van Patton was superbly coached by Harry Litwack. They were among the top-ranked college teams in the country.

Interest in the Big 5 had reached a crescendo pitch for the deciding game that first season. Both teams were 3-0 and the Palestra was packed. Before the game, the Hawk mascot flapped its wings and circled the court, taunted by his Owl counterpart.

Inside the locker room as I gave last-minute instructions to the team, we heard the Hawks' big drum booming its incessant beat, the Temple faithful roaring, "The Hawk is Dead" and the loyal St. Joe-ers, who had marched en masse from campus to the Palestra, predictably responding, "The Hawk will Never Die." The noise level, even in those cramped quarters under the stands, was deafening.

As the teams appeared for warmups, the crowd roared louder, and confetti filled the air. Then came the roll-outs for both sides — printed messages on large paper, unfurled to either proclaim the virtues of one team or playfully attack the other. Some were hilarious, others of questionable taste —but they always contributed to the high anticipation of what was to come.

The Hawks somehow managed to defuse the lightning-quick Lear-Rodgers connection, and find enough seams in The Chief's vaunted combination zone defense to squeeze out an upset win that night — one of the most exhilarating of my coaching life. But it was to become more than just a championship game.

The first Big 5 finale was the start of a tradition that has continued to the present day —that a Big 5 game means more in the Philadelphia area than national ranking; and no team — no matter how strong — is incapable of being upset by a local underdog rival.

Big 5 rivalries were so intense at that time, that winning those games was more important to me than any other team accomplishment. If I had a choice of coaching my team to either the Big 5 title or the national championship — but not both — I would have taken the former in a heartbeat.

I coached 11 years at St. Joseph's and have a flood of recollections that center around the Big 5. First was the participation of those who played for me —too numerous to mention here. But beginning with that first group in 1955, and ending with my best team —Matt Guokas, Cliff Anderson, Tom Duff, Marty Ford and Billy Oakes —11 years later, were some exceptional young men who shared with me the excitement and passion for playing Big 5 basketball at the Palestra. It was truly something special in our lives.

For all the intensity of the games and rivalries, and the potentially volatile Palestra setting—where highly partisan crowds could easily spill onto the floor—a high level of sportsmanship prevailed. The players and coaches respected each other, and despite all-out, aggressive play, there was never a fight nor the exchange of bitter words during the years I coached. It was what college sport is all about.

Then there were the by-products of those games. The games became a major event on campus. Each school continued to play some games in their own gyms, but the big ones were played at the Palestra. St. Joseph's always had a tradition of staunch support of its basketball team, but Big 5 competition fanned the flame to unprecedented heat. It became the embodiment of school spirit, that embraced the faculty as well as the student body. The Palestra became its focal point.

The Big 5 developed a heightened awareness of college basketball in the Delaware Valley. All doubleheaders were televised, where play-by-play man Les Keiter gave the game added zest with his special lingo, such as "ringtailed howitzer" (a long shot at the hoop), and "in-again, out-again Finnegan" (a shot that rimmed out). Big 5 basketball became THE winter sporting event of the Philadelphia area, especially since the Warriors had moved to San Francisco, and the 76ers had not yet made their appearance on the scene.

Weekly luncheons hosted by the Philadelphia Basketball Writers were held at the Sheraton Hotel, then located on 39th Street. The principals of that group —Bob Vetrone, Herb Good and Stan Hochman, loved the college game and promoted it well in their daily columns. They honored the Big 5 and small college Player of the Week at these luncheons, and then listened while each coach recounted the glories or woes of the previous week or foretold the colleagues of games ahead.

The coaches were a close, friendly group in that first year (Al Severance, Villanova; Ray Stanley, Penn; Hall of Fame player Jim Pollard, La Salle; Harry and me), and a tradition was set for those who followed. Everyone loved to hear the respected Litwack, and were intrigued and often amused by an impassioned discourse from Severance, the Main Line magistrate. My friend and former Eastern League teammate, Jack McCloskey, then an assistant at Penn, and I enjoyed exchanging friendly barbs. It was great fun.

At every luncheon, at least one of the teams seemed to have achieved something significant to celebrate and everyone was happy for another's success. The rivalries were intense, but the spirit of the group was always warm with genuine feelings of good will.

Some great coaching careers were forged in the cauldron of Big 5 competition. Litwack, Severance, McCloskey, Chuck Daly, Jack Kraft, Dudey Moore, Rollie Massimino, Don Casey, Bob Weinhauer, Dick Harter; and several who played for me—Jack McKinney, Jim Lynam, Jim Boyle and Paul Westhead — all earned their credentials in the coaching profession there.

And even the current group, including John Chaney (Temple), Fran Dunphy (Penn), Speedy Morris (La Salle), Steve Lappas (Villanova) and Phil Martelli (St. Joseph's) has felt the pressure to win those special games and the thrill of striving for a Big 5 title—although those games have lost some of their original luster.

The Big 5 changed over the years. Conference play is more important now. Villanova is in the Big East; Temple, St. Joseph's and La Salle are in the expanded Atlantic 10; Penn remains in the Ivy League. Because of conference demands, teams no longer play each other every year, and games have been moved from the Palestra to the larger capacity Spectrum or home team field houses. It's not the same.

There was something magical about the Palestra that can't be recaptured in other venues. And, when each team played a four-game Big 5 series every year, they were the games coaches underlined when the schedules came out, and players planned for in their summer workouts.

That's how it was when the Big 5 first started. It was a special part of my life.

Donald Hunt's fine book has rekindled the wonderful memories of a unique period in the annals of college basketball.

Jack Ramsay
Big 5 Hall of Famer

THE PALESTRA

The home of the Big 5 from 1955 to 1986, the Palestra, known to some as "The Big House," was the place where the local teams scored thrilling upsets over national powers and played emotional City Series games.

The most storied gymnasium in the country, the Palestra has hosted more college games, more visiting teams and more NCAA tournaments than any other facility. Located on Penn's campus, the Palestra was given its name by Greek professor Dr. William N. Bates. In ancient Greece, young men would compete in a variety of events in a rectangular enclosure attached to the gymnasium—a "Palestra"—in full view of the audience.

> "I don't know how to explain it. This is a basketball cathedral."
> —Dick Weiss, *New York Daily News*, on the Palestra

The Temple Owls cheerleaders in action during a Big 5 game at the Palestra. *Photo by Ed Mahan*

NCAA DIVISION I OLDEST BUILDINGS

School, location, capacity, year established

Northeastern University, Boston, Mass.
Matthews Arena (6,000) est. 1909

Fordham University, Bronx, N.Y.
Rose Hill Gym (3,200) est. 1924

Harvard University, Cambridge, Mass.
Briggs Athletic Center (3,000) est. 1926

University of Oregon, Eugene, Ore.
McArthur Court (10,063) est. 1926

University of Pennsylvania, Philadelphia, Pa., Palestra (8,700) est. 1927

University of Washington, Seattle, Wash.
Edmundson Pavilion (8,000) est. 1927

Butler University, Indianapolis, Ind.
Hinkle Fieldhouse (11,000), est. 1928

University of Minnesota, Minneapolis, Minn. Williams Arena (14,395) est. 1928

*Penn State University, University Park, Pa., Rec Hall (6,846) est. 1929

University of Wisconsin, Madison, Wis.
Wisconsin Fieldhouse (11,500) est. 1930

*Penn State no longer plays in Rec Hall.

MOST POINTS, BIG 5

Individual:
Ken Durrett, La Salle, scored 45 points (vs. Western Kentucky) January 16, 1971.

Most Points, Opponent Individual:
Calvin Murphy, Niagara, scored 52 points (vs. La Salle) December 16, 1967.

Free Throws Made, Big 5 Individual:
Tom Sienkiewicz, Villanova, made 21 free throws (vs. Pennsylvania) February 13, 1979.

Free Throws Made, Opponent Individuals:
Jim McClellan, St. Francis of Loretto, made 18 (vs. St. Joseph's) December 11, 1957. Jim Morgan, Yale, made 18 (vs. Pennsylvania) February 22, 1969.

Most Rebounds, Big 5 Individual:
Clifford Anderson, St. Joseph's grabbed 32 (vs. La Salle) February 26, 1967.

Most Rebounds, Opponent Individual:
Spencer Haywood, Detroit, grabbed 32 (vs. La Salle) February 21, 1969.

"This is a place with magic in the air. The Palestra has the acoustics of a big bass drum. It's a basketball echo chamber where every sound is amplified, where 100 people sound like 1,000, where 1,000 sound like 10,000 and where 10,000 sound like nothing you've ever heard before.

"When the bleachers are full and the games are good, this is the best place to watch a college basketball game in America. There are other great gyms, other great crowds, certainly places where you'll see better teams. But they are not the Palestra . . . It is the best basketball gymnasium in the country—by far."

"The first time I ever walked into the Palestra, it was empty . . . I knew that was where I wanted to play." — *Dave Wohl, All-Big 5 point guard for Penn on the Palestra.*

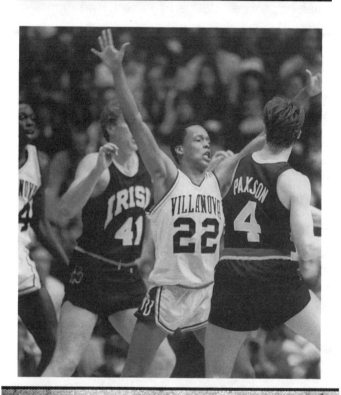

Villanova's Gary McLain (22) guards Notre Dame's John Paxson (4) during a non-conference game at the Palestra. McLain was the starting point guard on the Wildcats' 1985 national championship team. *Photo by Ed Mahan.*

The name "Palestra" was accepted by the organizing committee, for it fit the specifications of authenticity and dignity, while it was also descriptive and novel. So, in 1927, the Palestra was opened.

Since then, there have been many tributes to the glorious building, but no one has fallen more in love with the Palestra than Dallas-based sports writer Joe Rhoads, who, in 1985, covered college basketball games across the nation. Rhoads said:

PALESTRA RECORDS

Most Points, Game
128, St. Joseph's (Nevada Reno, 12/15/71)
52, Calvin Murphy, Niagara (La Salle, 12/16/76

Most Points, Big 5 Player
46, Bob Schafer, Villanova (Baldwin-Wallace, 1/8/54)

Most Points, Big 5 Game
117, Villanova (La Salle, 1/27/82)
39, Tom Sienkiewicz, Villanova (Penn, 2/13/79)

Most Points, Both Teams
216 (111-105), La Salle vs. Villanova (1/15/58)

Fewest Points, Both Teams
40 (28-12), Penn vs Swarthmore (1/10/34)

Widest Margin, Big Game
38 (104-66), La Salle vs. Villanova (2/20/74)

Most Field Goals Made
20, Ken Durrett, La Salle (Lafayette, 2/4/70)

Most Free Throws Made
21, Tom Sienkiewicz, Villanova (Penn, 2/13/79)

Most Free Throws Attempted
23, Tom Sienkiewicz, Villanova (Penn, 2/13/79)

Most Rebounds
34, Fred Cohen, Temple (Connecticut, 3/16/56)

Most Rebounds, Big 5 Game
32, Cliff Anderson, St. Joe's (La Salle, 2/26/67)

Aside from more than 60 years of Penn basketball and more than 30 years of Big 5 doubleheaders, the building has hosted 51 NCAA tournament games as part of 20 national championship competitions. The Palestra was the site of the first NCAA Tournament in 1939.

"There's nothing like playing at the Palestra," said Jack Ramsay, former St. Joseph's head coach. "I've been involved with a lot of great basketball games in the Big 5. The Palestra is a special place. The fans are right on top of you. It's a very loud building. Plus, when you have two local teams playing in the Big 5, the atmosphere is unbelievable."

"The Palestra didn't have theater seats, just those bleachers with everyone crowded in. You sat there rubbing shoulders with the guy next to you, and the human electricity got the place flowing." — *George Raveling, former Villanova assistant on the Palestra.*

Villanova's Kenny Wilson and St. Joseph's Wayne Williams embrace after a Big 5 game at the Palestra. The Villanova-St. Joseph's rivalry has been one of the most heated in Big 5 history. *Photo by Ed Mahan.*

Villanova players and fans celebrate after a big win over Notre Dame at the Palestra. *Photo by Ed Mahan.*

NCAAA TOURNAMENTS AT THE PALESTRA

1939	Eastern Championship
1954	Eastern Regional
1955	Eastern Regional
1956	Eastern Regional
1957	Eastern Regional
1962	First Round
1963	First Round, Eastern Regional
1964	First Round
1965	First Round
1970	First Round
1971	First Round
1973	First Round
1974	First Round
1975	First Round
1977	First Round
1978	First Round
1983	Opening Round
1984	Opening Round
1986	Women's Opening Round
1991	Women's Eastern Regional

Ed Pinckney, who led Villanova to the 1985 NCAA championship over Georgetown, remembers all of the heated Big 5 rivalries at the Palestra. Pinckney feels there aren't many buildings in college basketball like the one on Penn's campus.

"The Palestra may be old," said Pinckney, who has played 10 years in the NBA, "but there's nothing like it. I didn't know a lot about the Palestra because I'm from New York. But I found out very quickly. The place just rocks when it's crowded. I really enjoyed playing the Big 5 games in the Palestra. Villanova had some great games against Temple, St. Joseph's, La Salle and all the city schools. Plus, we played some Big East and non-conference games there too. And you know what? We always had great attendance."

Jerome Allen, former Penn standout, didn't play all of his Big 5 games at the Palestra. But Allen played most of his college basketball games there.

"I'll always remember playing Big 5 games at the Palestra," Allen said. "These games were against a lot of my friends from high school, the Sonny Hill League and the Philadelphia basketball commu-

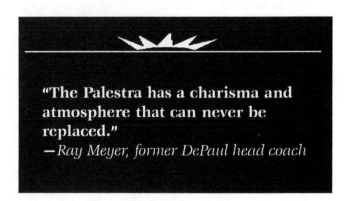

St. Joseph's fans celebrate as they defeat Villanova, 60-59 to win the Big 5 City Series championship at the Palestra in 1980. *Photo by Ed Mahan.*

nity. I'm fortunate to not only play Big 5 games at the Palestra, but Ivy League games as well. The Penn-Princeton matchup was always a big game at the Palestra. When we played against Princeton at the Palestra, we always had a homecourt advantage because of the crowd, noise and excitement."

There have been a lot of great performances at The Palestra over the years. The Big 5 has seen some of the finest players in the history of college basketball such as Wilt Chamberlain, Jerry West and Oscar Robertson. On the following page are some of the best performances at the Palestra.

"The Palestra has a charisma and atmosphere that can never be replaced."
—*Ray Meyer, former DePaul head coach*

GREAT PERFORMANCES AT THE PALESTRA

SINCE THE 1955-56 SEASON . . .

There have been many great performances at The Palestra over the years. The Big 5 has seen some of the finest players in the history of college basketball, including Wilt Chamberlain, Jerry West, and Oscar Robertson. Following are some of the best performances at The Palestra.

MOST POINTS, BIG 5 INDIVIDUAL:

Ken Durrett, La Salle, scored 45 points (vs. Western Kentucky) January 16, 1971.

MOST POINTS, OPPONENT:

Individual: Calvin Murphy, Niagara, scored 52 points (vs. La Salle) December 16, 1967.

FREE THROWS MADE, BIG 5 INDIVIDUAL:

Tom Sienkiewicz, Villanova, made 21 free throws, vs. Pennsylvania) February 13, 1979.

FREE THROWS MADE, OPPONENT INDIVIDUAL:

Jim McClellan, St. Francis of Loretto, made 18 (vs. St. Joseph's) December 11, 1957.
Jim Morgan, Yale, made 18 (vs. Pennsylvania) February 22, 1969.

MOST REBOUNDS, BIG 5 INDIVIDUAL:

Clifford Anderson, St. Joseph's, grabbed 32 (vs. La Salle) February 26, 1967.

MOST REBOUNDS, OPPONENT INDIVIDUAL:

Spencer Haywood, Detroit, grabbed 32 (vs. La Salle) February 21, 1969.

MEMORIES OF THE PALESTRA . . .

Rollie Massimino's staff, fans and players celebrate in a game against Georgetown at the Palestra. *Photo by Ed Mahan.*

The Villanova Wildcat and a majorette perform during a Big 5 game against St. Joseph's at the Palestra. *Photo by Ed Mahan.*

"The depth perception is so good that you could almost reach out and touch the basket."
—*former Louisville star Jeff Hall*

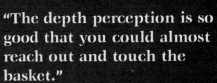

The La Salle cheerleaders take a break during Big 5 action at the Palestra. *Photo by Ed Mahan.*

The St. Joseph's Hawk and the Temple Owls' mascot meet the Phillie Phanatic during halftime of their Big 5 game at the Palestra. Photo by Ed Mahan.

During World War II, Penn was bumped from the Palestra by the Navy and began participating in the Convention Hall doubleheaders.

Penn's cheerleaders perform before a soldout crowd at the Palestra. Photo by Ed Mahan.

A soldout crowd watches Big 5 action at the Palestra. In addition to Big 5 games, the Palestra has hosted NCAA tournament games and some of the finest college basketball teams in the country. Big 5 teams have played against such college basketball powerhouses as North Carolina, Duke, Louisville and Georgetown at the Palestra.

"The best thing about the Palestra is its intimacy . . . When you watch a game at the Palestra, you become more than a spectator—you become a participant." — *Mike Stanton, Basketball Weekly*

THE HISTORY OF THE BIG 5

The Philadelphia Big 5 has one of the most unique college basketball traditions in the country. The Big 5 is comprised of five colleges in the Philadelphia area—Temple University, La Salle University, the University of Pennsylvania, Villanova University and St. Joseph's University. For more than 40 years, these five illustrious city schools have been battling each other for the City Championship. These highly anticipated games carry great importance among coaches, players and fans of the local schools.

George Bertelsman was one of the athletic directors instrumental in the formation of the Big 5. Bertelsman was athletic director at St. Joseph's.

The formation of the Big 5 was conceived by Penn athletic director Jerry Ford, who discussed the concept with the other athletic directors. Bob Paul, Penn's sports information director, and John Rossiter, the Quakers' business manager, put the round-robin format together. The other athletic directors involved in the Big 5's inception were La Salle's Jim Henry, St. Joseph's George Bertelsman, Temple's Josh Cody and Villanova's Ambrose (Bud) Dudley.

Penn and Villanova had been hosting Saturday night doubleheaders in the Palestra, while Temple, La Salle and St. Joseph's played competing twinbills in Convention Hall, only three blocks away. The Convention Hall three had their own title city series; while Penn and Villanova did not even play one another. Tom Gola, Bill Mlkvy and George Senesky never played Penn or Villanova. Paul Arizin and Ernie Beck never faced La Salle, St. Joseph's and Temple.

The official announcement of the formation of the Big 5 was made by University of Pennsylvania president Dr. Gaylord Harnwell at Penn's Houston Hall on November 23, 1954. The Big 5 was touted as a chance for Philadelphia to present the best basketball it had to offer with the schools sharing the profits evenly after Penn was paid for Palestra upkeep. As a unit, the five were about to secure a television contract.

Joining Penn's Harnwell for the historic Big 5 announcement were the school presidents—Rev. Very Edward G. Jacklin, St. Joseph's; Temple's Dr. Robert Johnson; Villanova's Very Rev. James A. Donellon, O.S.A.; and La Salle's Rev. Brother Erminus Stanisiaus. The agreement reached by the esteemed leaders of these five schools has provided much exciting basketball for many Philadelphia

THE FIRST ALL-BIG 5 TEAM

1955-56
First Team

Dick Censits, Penn

Kurt Engelbert, St. Joseph's

Mike Fallon, St. Joseph's

Al Juliana, St. Joseph's

Hal Lear, Temple

Bill Lynch, St. Joseph's

Fran O'Malley, La Salle

Hal Reinfeld, Temple

*Guy Rodgers, Temple

Jimmy Smith, Villanova

Joe Sturgis, Penn

*MVP

In June 1986, the presidents of the five colleges signed a 10-year contract to continue the round-robin format at each school's respective gymnasium. In the 1991-92 season, the format was changed, and currently each team plays one Big 5 game at home and one on the road each year. Penn, La Salle, St. Joseph's and Temple play one another every season, regardless of whether the games count in City Series standings.

In the 60s, the biggest City Series matchup was Villanova and St. Joseph's. This rivalry featured some marvelous players, including Villanova's Wali Jones, Jim Washington, and Hubie White; and St. Joseph's Jim Lynam, Tom Wynne, Matt Guokas, Cliff Anderson and Mike Hauer. Temple won the National Invitation Tournament by defeating Boston College, 89-76 in 1969. La Salle's 23-1 team was one of the finest college teams in Big 5 history. Unfortunately, the Explorers were not allowed to participate in the NCAA tournament because of an NCAA violation.

When St. Joseph's beat La Salle, 97-85, on January 9, 1957, it was the first overtime game in Big 5 history.

fans. Each decade since has boasted many terrific games and outstanding moments in Big 5 history.

The first Big 5 doubleheader was held on December 3, 1955 at the Palestra on the campus of the University of Pennsylvania. That night, Muhlenberg defeated La Salle, 69-58, and St. Joseph's spanked Rhode Island, 84-72. St. Joseph's beat Villanova, 83-70, in their first Big 5 game on December 14, 1955.

This historic alliance has produced some fierce rivalries, huge upsets, and great players. Fans have travelled across the city to watch Philadelphia college basketball at the Palestra; the official home of the Big 5 from 1955-86. This storied facility has hosted more college basketball games than any other in the country.

The 70s produced three sensational Big 5 teams. In 1971, Villanova lost to UCLA, 68-62 in the NCAA championship game. That same year, Dick Harter's Penn Quakers finished the season with an amazing 28-1 record. In 1979, Bob Weinhauer's Penn Quakers lost to Magic Johnson's Michigan State Spartans in the NCAA Final Four. Penn was the dominant team of the decade, winning seven Big 5 championships. La Salle's Michael Brooks was a consensus first-team All American and was the United States Basketball Writers "Player of the Year"

1955-56 BIG 5 TEAMS IN POSTSEASON PLAY

Temple (NCAA Tournament):

Temple defeated Holy Cross, 74-72; Connecticut, 75-9; Canisius, 60-58; lost to Iowa, 83-76; defeated Southern Methodist, 90-81. Finished third place in the tournament.

St Joseph's (NIT):

St Joseph's defeated Seton Hall, 74-65; lost to Louisville, 89-79; defeated St. Francis of New York, 93-82.

Joseph's) and Julie Reidenauer (La Salle) composed the first class to be inducted into the women's Big 5 Hall of Fame.

In 1990, La Salle's Lionel Simmons was named college basketball's Player of the Year. In 1993, Temple made its third trip to the NCAA Final Eight losing to Michigan, 77-72, a team that featured NBA players Chris Webber, Juwan Howard and Jalen Rose. The Owls' famous tandem of Eddie Jones and Aaron McKie were both first-round picks of the Los Angeles Lakers and the Portland Trail Blazers respectively. In 1995, La Salle joined Temple and St. Joseph's in the Atlantic 10 Conference. Villanova became the first non-conference team to defeat the University of North Carolina twice in one season.

In spite of the demands of conference play, preseason tournaments and national television, the Big 5 schools have agreed to a new 10-year contract that will allow the schools to continue to play each other for the City Series championship into

in 1979. That was also the same year the Big 5 schools decided to expand the round-robin play to crown a city champion for the women as well as the men.

In the 80s, Villanova moved to center stage as it defeated Dayton, Michigan, Maryland, North Carolina, Memphis State and Georgetown to win the 1985 NCAA title. The Wildcats, coached by Rollie Massimino were led by Ed Pinckney, Dwayne McClain and Gary McLain.

In 1988, Temple finished the regular season ranked No. 1 in college basketball. The Owls advanced to the NCAA Final Eight before losing to Duke, 63-53. John Chaney, the Owls' head coach, was named National Coach of the Year. Temple and Villanova weren't the only schools to receive national recognition during this decade. La Salle's Lionel Simmons led the Explorers to the NIT finals before losing to Southern Mississippi, 94-80.

In 1989, Lynn Blaszczk (Temple), Sharon Gross (Penn), Karen Hiznay (Villanova), Muffet O'Brien (St.

In February 1995, La Salle joined Big 5 opponents Temple and St. Joseph's in the Atlantic 10 Conference.

the next decade. The new contract will be the same as the last one; each team will play two City Series games a season.

On June 6, 1986 the Big 5 schools inked a 10-year contract to discontinue playing the games at the Palestra and instead host them in the respective campus gymnasiums. Traditional Big 5 fans were upset with the arrangement, but the City Series games were still intact. All five schools played each other every season in a City Series game. In May 1991, the Big 5 went to a half round-robin format.

THE CITY OF
PHILADELPHIA

Philadelphia, the nation's fifth-largest city, is known as a center of culture and history and as a leader in science and commerce. The city's Independence Park is regarded as "America's most historic square mile." The park's Independence Hall and Liberty Bell are two of the most recognizable attractions in our country.

Philadelphia boasts the nation's first zoo, which houses 1,600 animals on 42 beautiful acres. The first U.S. mint was also built in Philadelphia in 1792; it is still the largest mint in the world.

Philadelphia is a living, breathing museum, offering dozens of cultural opportunities. There are 20 major museums including the world-renowned Museum of Art and the Rodin Museum. Many theater productions make Philadelphia their last

Many residents and tourists travel the Benjamin Franklin Parkway in Philadelphia. *Photo by Robert Coldwell.*

Philadelphia boasts one of the country's largest concentrations of colleges, with over 30 campuses located within a 15-mile radius.

A view of the Benjamin Franklin Parkway leading to Center City, Philadelphia. *Photo by Robert Coldwell.*

A view of the William Penn Statue and City Hall. *Photo by Robert Coldwell.*

Philadelphia is as diverse as its people, who come from all races and religions: the Italian market, Chinatown, the Korean shops on Fifth Street and the Latino "Street of Gold."

stop before hitting Broadway. Nightlife includes cuisine from around the globe, waterfront night-clubs and dozens of movie theaters.

Unquestionably recognized for some of the world's leading cultural institutions, Philadelphia is especially proud of its Academy of Music, the oldest opera house in the nation (1857) and the home of the incomparable Philadelphia Orchestra. The Academy hosts performances by the Opera Company of Philadelphia and the Pennsylvania Ballet.

In addition to history, fine arts and other activities, Philadelphia is home to six professional sports teams: the Phillies (baseball), the Sixers (basketball), the Eagles (football), the Flyers (hockey) the Wings (lacrosse), and the Bulldogs (roller hockey). The Phillies and Eagles play in Veterans Stadium and CoreStates Center is the new home of the 76ers and Flyers. Finally, Philadelphia is the home of Big 5 basketball.

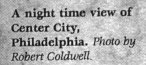

A night time view of Center City, Philadelphia. *Photo by Robert Coldwell.*

TEMPLE UNIVERSITY

S ince the University was founded by Russell Conwell in 1884, Temple has preserved, as well as fulfilled, its mission of providing opportunity with excellence for generations of deserving students. People of all cultural, religious, racial, physical and economic backgrounds come to study, teach, conduct research and work at Temple University. Under the leadership of President Peter J. Liacouras, Temple is rapidly becoming one of the country's most comprehensive research universities. A member of the Commonwealth System of Higher Education since 1965, the University has 32,000 students and some 2,000 faculty. It offers bachelor's degrees in 107 areas, master's degrees in 88 fields, 66 doctoral degrees and first professional degrees in five areas. Fourteen schools and colleges make up

Temple University President Peter J. Liacouras is in his 14th year as chief executive officer.

Temple University Director of Athletics David P. O'Brien.

the University and are located on five campuses in the greater Philadelphia area. The 94.5-acre main campus is located approximately one mile north of Center City, Philadelphia, and is a vibrant campus crisscrossed with tree-lined walkways that lead past ivy-covered and modern buildings.

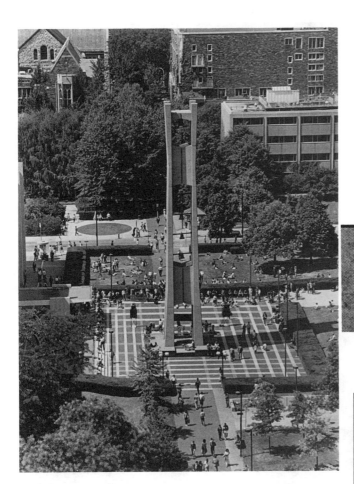

Temple faculty members have won prestigious recognition for the quality of their instruction—including the Lindback Award, Fulbright, Guggenheim and Carnegie grants, as well as Temple's own Great Teacher Award.

The Bell Tower is the central meeting place for students on Temple University's Main Campus. More than 30,000 full-time and part-time undergraduate, graduate and professional students attend Temple.

Temple is one of Pennsylvania's four Commonwealth universities, along with Penn State, Pitt, and Lincoln.

A Temple cheerleading squad inspires the crowd.

THE APOLLO IN THE MAKING

City representatives, neighborhood people and staff members from Temple University united on January 25, 1996 to celebrate the beginning of construction of the largest building project in North Philadelphia in a long time. On that day, the ground breaking was held for The Apollo of Temple. Quite naturally, it was a great day for Temple.

Scheduled to open in December of 1997, The Apollo will be the new home for John Chaney and the Temple Owls basketball team. The Apollo, a three-building complex that includes a Convocation center and a Recreation/Community Center, will rise on the 1700 block of North Broad Street. An Entertainment/Parking Center, on the west side of 15th Street and connected to the Convocation Center via enclosed pedestrian bridge, will break ground in the near future.

Apollo was the Greco-Roman god of light, music, poetry, sport and healing. He was a paradigm of youthful beauty. Taking a cue from its namesake, the Apollo project has been designed as a venue for culture, sports, entertainment, commerce, and education.

The Convocation Center will seat 11,000 for convocations, commencements, and concerts; 10,200 for basketball games; 9,000 for indoor soccer; 8,000 for tennis matches and up to 3,500 for dance and theater. (The theater configuration is named for benefactress Esther Boyer Griswold.) And since the facility will be fully marketed for events outside the University, it, along with Temple's Rock Hall, will serve as a major

resource for the city in its much ballyhooed Avenue of the Arts North.

The adjacent Recreation/Community Center will house a host of activities including aerobics, general

At the ground breaking ceremony on January 25, 1996, President Peter J. Liacouras, shovel in hand, was flanked by State Senator Vincent J. Fumo (left) and David L. Cohen, Chief of Staff to the mayor of Philadelphia (right).

fitness programs, racquetball, and a three-lane indoor 280-meter jogging track. It will also serve as a learning site of advanced technology for residents of the neighborhood who will have access to a community meeting room. Four retail stores will be in front on Cecil B. Moore Avenue.

The Entertainment/Parking Center will provide space for 1,200 cars. Plans are being made for additional retail stores and possibly a jazz club, a new home for WRTI — Temple's jazz radio network — and a multiscreen theater.

The site, which is bounded by Broad Street, Cecil B. Moore Avenue, 15th Street and Montgomery Avenue, is being prepared for the $85 million Apollo of Temple.

UNIVERSITY OF PENNSYLVANIA

Founded by Benjamin Franklin in 1740, the University of Pennsylvania is the fourth oldest college in the country. The University of Pennsylvania is located along the west bank of the Schuylkill River, less than two miles from the center of Philadelphia. The campus comprises 260 acres and 119 buildings in West Philadelphia.

The University of Pennsylvania is composed of four undergraduate schools and 12 graduate and professional schools on a single campus.

The first collegiate school of business in the United States was the Wharton School of Finance and Commerce founded in 1881. The first University-owned teaching hospital, the Hospital of the University of Pennsylvania, was founded in 1874. The world's first large-scale, all-electronic, general purpose digital computer, the ENIAC, was completed at Penn in 1946.

Academic diversity and a nationally acclaimed faculty are found in 53 departments of the four undergraduate schools.

University of Pennsylvania President Judith Rodin is the first Penn alumna to be named president.

The 1994 Penn cheerleaders.

Pennsylvania's undergraduate enrollment is just over 9,800. Students come from all 50 states and foreign countries. Currently, 57 percent of the student body are men and 34 percent racial minorities. The student-faculty ratio is seven-to-one. Measures of distinction include several Nobel Prizes in the past two decades, numerous Pulitzer Prizes and more than 160 Guggenheim Fellowships.

Penn's College Hall.

Rick Miller, the 1993-94 Penn mascot.

College basketball using five-man teams was first initiated in an 1897 Penn-Yale game.

The Wharton School is considered the top-rated undergraduate business school in the world, excelling in finance, real estate, entrepreneurship, and insurance/risk management.

ST. JOSEPH'S

St. Joseph's is a nationally recognized, private Jesuit university, located on the western boundary of Philadelphia. St. Joseph's strives for excellence and balance in its academic programs, all within the framework of the Jesuit tradition of service to others. The 60-acre campus combines urban accessibility with the charm of the suburban Main Line. With 2,700 full-time undergraduates, St. Joseph's offers an intimate community atmosphere with numerous opportunities for student leadership. Additionally, the average class size of 25 and a faculty/student ratio of 15:1 allows for personal mentoring and easy access to professors.

St. Joseph's University President Rev. Nicholas S. Rashford, S.J. is in his tenth year at St. Joseph's helm.

Don DiJulia was named Assistant Vice-President and Athletic Director at St. Joseph's in 1988.

St. Joseph's remains dedicated to its founding principle: that a liberal arts-based education teaches disciplined reasoning, effective communication and a love of learning. The scope of St. Joseph's academic programs, technology and facilities equals those of larger schools. It is this academic excellence that has earned St. Joseph's accolades across the nation.

The most decorated mascot in the country, The Hawk has garnered numerous accolades in its 40-year history. It has been selected the nation's top mascot by *Sports Illustrated*, *Street & Smith Basketball Yearbook* and *ESPN College Basketball* magazine.

St. Joseph's is proud of its singular status as Philadelphia's Jesuit University. The university's commitment to teaching is what distinguishes St. Joseph's from other colleges and universities.

VILLANOVA UNIVERSITY

F ounded in 1848 as a small Augustinian private college for men, today Villanova University's enrollment is well over 6,000 full-time undergraduates, including male and female students from many parts of the world. Originally known as Villanova College, the university was organized by and is under the direction of the Order of St. Augustine, better known as the Augustinian Friars, one of the oldest religious teaching orders of the Roman Catholic Church.

The full-time faculty, numbering over 500, teach both graduates and undergraduates. Small classes are the norm at Villanova, which has an advantageous student/teacher ratio of 12:1. The

Rev. Edmund J. Dobbin, O.S.A., was named the 31st President of Villanova University on September 1, 1988.

Villanova University Director of Athletics Gene DeFilippo has rebuilt nearly every phase of Villanova athletics in his short tenure.

excellence of Villanova's academic programs is attested to by its strong faculty—90 percent of whom hold doctoral degrees—and by the presence of such prestigious academic societies as a chapter of Phi Beta Kappa.

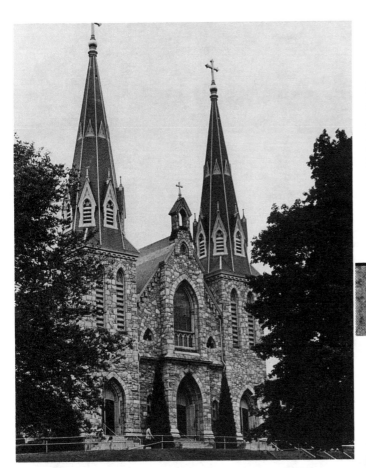

Twelve miles west of Philadelphia, Villanova is located on 222 handsomely landscaped acres on the Main Line, a corridor of prestigious residential areas. The picturesque campus is comprised of more than 50 buildings ranging from traditional gray stone to modern steel and glass.

Villanova Chapel,
Villanova University

Villanova's distinguished alumni include seven state Supreme Court Justices, members of Congress, White House staff members, mayors of major American cities, and bishops of the Roman Catholic Church, among many others.

The 1994 Villanova
University cheerleaders.
Photo by Stephen C. Augsberger.

LA SALLE UNIVERSITY

L a Salle is a comprehensive university that combines the best of all educational worlds. With more than 5,700 men and women attending classes, the university offers a pleasant environment in close proximity to Philadelphia's cultural, social and historic centers.

Founded by the Brothers of the Christian Schools in 1863, La Salle is named for St. John Baptist de La Salle, who established the Christian Brothers teaching order 300 years ago. The institution, which began as a one-building academy in Center City, Philadelphia, is on a 100-acre, 43-building campus adjacent to Philadelphia's Germantown section.

The La Salle day and evening faculty numbers 400. With a student-faculty ratio of 14-1 and

Brother Joseph F. Burke, F.S.C., Ph.D., became La Salle University's 27th president on July 1, 1992.

Under the direction of La Salle Director of Athletics Robert Mullen, the Explorers men's and women's basketball programs have achieved national recognition.

an average class size of 20, students can be assured of as much personal guidance as they need. This commitment to the individual student has always been a major tenet of the Christian Brothers.

La Salle students come from 26 states and 20 foreign countries. The university has enjoyed increased national attention in recent years, including being named by *U.S.News & World Report* as one of the country's leading regional universities in 1993, 1994, and 1995.

La Salle University cheerleaders.

A nationwide study of nearly 900 private undergraduate institutions ranked La Salle in the top four percent since 1977 as an originating school for Ph.D.s.

La Salle's mascot, "The Explorer."

THE BIG 5'S GREATEST TEAMS

Over the years, there have been many talented teams in the Big 5. Sometimes the most talented teams don't live up to expectations, and occasionally, average teams rise above adversity or just simply play better when the pressure is on—the postseason does that to some teams. The Big 5 is usually well represented come March Madness. No other city has sent more teams into postseason play than Philadelphia. In 1995 Penn, Temple, and Villanova played in the NCAA tournament and St. Joseph's participated in the NIT. Drexel also earned a bid to the NCAA tournament in 1995. That was five Philadelphia teams that came down with a bad case of March Madness. During that exciting time, the college basketball frenzy sets in across the city of Philadelphia. Fans everywhere were glued to their television sets watching their favorite local teams play.

VILLANOVA'S 1985 NCAA CHAMPIONSHIP TEAM

The 1985 Villanova Wildcats were an unlikely pick to win a national championship. They lost their final regular season game to Pitt, 85-62, and finished with a 25-10 record overall.

Villanova's starting frontcourt included 6-9 Ed Pinckney, 6-7 Harold Pressley, and 6-5 Dwayne McClain. The backcourt starters were 6-2 Dwight Wilbur and 6-0 Gary McLain. Coach Rollie Massimino's top reserves were 6-5 Harold Jensen and 6-5 Mark Plansky.

Of all these players, only Pinckney has had a successful career in the NBA. Pressley, a first-round pick of the Sacramento Kings, played four seasons in the NBA before going to play overseas, and McClain lasted one season with the Indiana Pacers.

Ed Pinckney earned MVP honors of the 1985 NCAA Final Four. Pinckney scored 16 points to help guide the Wildcats to the title.

Nevertheless, when it came time to play in the postseason, Villanova was well prepared. Massimino had the ability to get the most out of his players and a reputation for having his teams ready to play in the NCAA tournament.

**1984-85 Villanova University Wildcats
NCAA National Champions**

Sitting, left to right: Dwight Wilbur, Veltra Dawson, R.C. Massimino, Gary McLain, Brian Harrington, Harold Jensen, Steve Pinone. Standing, left to right: Wyatt Maker, Ed Pinckney, Mark Plansky, Harold Pressley, Coach Roland V. Massimino, Dwayne McClain, Connally Brown, Chuck Everson. Photo by Villanova University Media Relations.

In the 1985 NCAA tournament, Villanova neutralized its opponents' top players. In the Wildcats' wins over Dayton (51-49), Michigan (59-55), Maryland (46-43), North Carolina (56-44), Memphis State (52-45) and Georgetown (66-64), Massimino constantly changed defenses, keeping teams off balance. He received some major contributions from McLain and Jensen; McLain shut down Michigan's Gary Grant and Georgetown's Michael Jackson, and Jensen replaced Wilbur in the championship game and shot an incredible 5-for-5 from the field and 4-for-5 from the free throw line for 14 in the big victory over Georgetown.

Pinckney, McClain, and Pressley were the team's stars, but Wilbur, Jensen, McLain, and Plansky raised the level of their play when they were most needed.

Against Georgetown, the Wildcats played an almost perfect game. Villanova hit 22 of 28 field goal attempts for an amazing 78.6 percent. In the second half, the Wildcats connected on nine of 10 field goals. From the free throw line, Villanova was 22 of 27, including 11 of 14 in the final two minutes.

Pinckney, who scored 16 points and grabbed six rebounds against Patrick Ewing, still remembers the great moments.

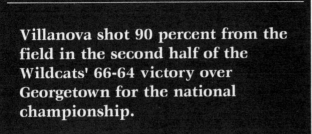

Villanova shot 90 percent from the field in the second half of the Wildcats' 66-64 victory over Georgetown for the national championship.

"The win over Georgetown for the national championship will always be something special," Pinckney said. "I know a lot of people didn't think we could pull it off. But we were able to get it done. That was the year when we came through in the big games. And that's a sign of a true winner."

VILLANOVA: 1971 NCAA FINALIST

The 1971 Villanova Wildcats, 27-6 under head coach Jack Kraft, came very close to defeating No. 1-ranked UCLA for the national championship. The Bruins (28-1) were coached by the Wizard of Westwood, legendary John Wooden.

The Bruins were paced by Sidney Wicks, Curtis Rowe, Henry Bibby, and Steve Patterson. UCLA, heading into the 1971 championship game, had won four straight NCAA championships and six of the previous seven NCAA titles. UCLA had compiled a 144-5 record over five seasons, and

1970-71 Villanova Basketball Team

Eastern Champions and NCAA National Runner-Up

Kneeling left to right: Clarence Smith, Hank Siemiontkowski,

John Fox, head coach Jack Kraft, Howard Porter, Gary Jentz, Joe McDowell. Standing, left to right: Manager Tom Himes, asst. coach Dan Dougherty, Mike Daly, Bob Gohl, Ed Hastings, Chris Ford, Tom Ingelsby, Greg Newman, manager Larry Morgan, trainer Jake Nevin. Photo by Villanova University Media Relations.

the Bruins had won 27 straight NCAA tournament games. Kraft's team of only nine men peaked in the tournament. The Villanova "Iron Men" had plenty of talent.

The Wildcats were led by Howard Porter, Clarence Smith, Hank Siemiontkowski, Chris Ford, and Tom Ingelsby. This Villanova team had an incredible run in the tournament. They beat St. Joseph's (93-75) at the Palestra; beat Fordham (85-75) and Penn (90-47) in Raleigh, North Carolina; and defeated Western Kentucky (92-89) in the semifinals. Villanova's biggest win was over the Quakers. Penn (28-1) won the Big 5 that season and had beaten Villanova, 78-70, at The Palestra. The Wildcats' shocking victory margin of 43 points was incredible; the 90-47 score appeared on Villanova fans' shirts the next year.

> "Gimme Five" boldly exclaimed buttons worn by UCLA fans in the Houston Astrodome for the championship game. UCLA had run up an amazing 144-5 record dating back five seasons, and the Bruins had won 27 straight NCAA Tournament games.

Patterson scored 29 points and Bibby 17 as they led UCLA to the NCAA title with a 68-62 win over the Wildcats. Avid Villanova fans remember Howard Porter and Hank Siemiontkowski outplaying Wicks and Rowe in this exciting contest. Porter scored 25 points and pulled down eight rebounds, while Siemiontkowski tallied 19 points and grabbed six rebounds. Rowe scored eight points and had eight rebounds and Wicks finished with seven points and nine rebounds.

"It shows you what a good team can do," Kraft said. "You hold down Wicks and Rowe as well as we did, and that third guy kills you." The third guy was Patterson, who killed Villanova's chances of winning a national championship. But no one, including Patterson could ruin Villanova's outstanding season.

The crown tipped and wavered but did not fall. The dynasty lived on. In the loss, Villanova earned a consolation prize of sorts. The six-point victory spread was the narrowest among UCLA's seven title-clinching victories.

VILLANOVA WINS THE 1994 NATIONAL INVITATION TOURNAMENT TITLE

After two consecutive losing seasons, the Villanova Wildcats returned in 1994 in championship form under head coach Steve Lappas. This Villanova team featured four freshmen, four sophomores, and two juniors. Every preseason poll, preview magazine, and the Big East Conference Writers Alliance picked Villanova to finish last in the conference.

Lappas and his assistants realized early that they had the talent and chemistry to do better than expected, despite early losses to Temple, Florida, Arizona State, and Providence.

The Wildcats posted impressive Big East wins over Connecticut, Pittsburgh, Boston College, and Georgetown twice during the regular season. Villanova was paced by sophomores Kerry Kittles (19.7

1994 NIT Champion Villanova Wildcats. *Photo by Villanova University Media Relations.*

On March 30, 1994, Villanova became the 15th major college basketball program to win both an NCAA and NIT Championship, when the Wildcats defeated Vanderbilt 80-73 to take the NIT title. The Wildcats' championship run capped a season that surpassed all expectations.

ppg), Eric Eberz (12.6 ppg), junior Jonathan Haynes (11.7 ppg), and freshmen Jason Lawson (10.1 ppg, 6.6 rpg) and Alvin Williams (7.9 ppg).

Kittles earned All-Big East first-team honors (the first Wildcat to do so since Harold Pressley in 1986), while Lawson earned Big East All-Rookie Team honors. Kittles also earned all-league team and Most Improved Player honors from the Big East Writers Alliance and Eastern College Athletic Conference (ECAC) second team.

Villanova was eliminated from the Big East tournament by Providence in the first round, 77-66. The Wildcats' 15-12 record did not get them a bid to the NCAA tournament.

In the NIT, Villanova started off with a victory over Canisius, 103-79. The Wildcats scored over 100 points for the first time since 1990, had their highest point total since 1982, and won a postseason game for the first time since 1991.

Villanova then went to Pittsburgh and spanked Duquesne in the second round of the NIT, 82-66, behind Eberz's career-high 22. Haynes added 17, and Kittles and Williams each had 14 points. The win was Villanova's first second-round victory since 1988.

In the quarterfinal game against Xavier, Eberz hit a huge basket to give Villanova a 76-74 win. Eberz finished with 13 points, Kittles 19, Haynes 14 and Williams 11, but Lawson had 17 points and a career-high 15 rebounds.

At Madison Square Garden in New York, Villanova trimmed Siena, 66-58, before a hostile crowd in a semifinal game. The Wildcats received a game-high 21 points from Kittles, and 17 points and 13 rebounds from Williams. The victory catapulted Villanova into the NIT finals for the first time since 1965, and a matchup with Vanderbilt University.

In the championship game, Villanova trailed by 15 points at halftime. Haynes with 19 points, Kittles 18, and Eberz 16, as Villanova defeated Vanderbilt, 80-73 to win the NIT; Villanova's first NIT championship.

TEMPLE'S FIRST-EVER NO. 1 TEAM

Temple's 1987-88 team was the finest Big 5 team that didn't get to the Final Four. The Owls (32-2) were ranked No. 1 in the country in the final week of the regular season. No other Big 5 team has been No. 1 for even a week.

The 1987-88 Temple University Men's Basketball Team

Sitting left to right: assistant coach Jim Maloney, Tom Katsikis, Jerome Dowdell, Howard Evans, head coach John Chaney, Mark Macon, Shoun Randolph, Mike Vreeswyk, assistant coach Jay Norman, assistant coach Dean Demopoulos. Standing left to right: assistant business manager John DiSangro, manager Robert Jones, Ernest Pollard, Derrick Brantley, Tim Perry, Duane Causwell, Ramon Rivas, Shawn Johnson, Darrin Pearsall, student trainer Tom Collins, assistant trainer Roger Clark.

This team featured such great players as Tim Perry, Mark Macon, Howard Evans, Ramon Rivas, Mike Vreeswyk, and Duane Causwell; Perry was named the Atlantic 10 Player of the Year, and Macon was named National Freshman of the Year.

Howard Evans was one of the best playmakers in college basketball. Big 5 fans will never forget his performance against Villanova on February 10, 1988. That night he dished a school-record 20 assists, scored 17 points, hit nine of 10 free throws, grabbed six rebounds, had two steals and only one turnover in Temple's 98-86 win.

Ramon Rivas, a 6-11, 250-pound power forward/center, did a lot of dirty work. He set massive picks for Macon and Vreeswyk. He picked up some easy hoops around the basketball and played solid defense in the lane.

Mike Vreeswyk was a tremendous three-point shooter with great range. The fans at Temple's McGonigle Hall would yell "Threeswyk" in honor of his three-point marksmanship.

Duane Causwell, a 6-11 center, teamed up with 6-9 Tim Perry to give the Owls a terrific shotblocking combination. There weren't many players who would drive to the basket against these powerful Owls.

The Owls concluded the season with a record of 32-2, the best mark in school history. In the aftermath, Chaney was named National Coach of the Year for the second year in a row.

Temple posted some brilliant victories over UCLA, Villanova, North Carolina, and Georgetown. The Owls also won the Big 5 City Series and the Atlantic 10 regular season and tournament titles. Temple lost to Duke, however, in the East Region Final, 63-53. This was John Chaney's best team; with three players in the NBA from this team in Macon, Perry, and Causwell. Evans played in the CBA after an unsuccessful 76ers tryout. Rivas played a season with Boston, and has since prospered in Spain and with the Puerto Rico national teams. Vreeswyk, also an international star, got Eddie Jones to autograph Temple media guides for Mike's nephews, who didn't know Uncle Mike had more Owl points than Eddie Jones.

Temple's Howie Evans (21) set a school-record 20 assists, scored 17 points, hit nine of 10 free throws, grabbed six rebounds, had two steals and only one turnover in Temple's Big 5 victory over Villanova at McGonigle Hall on February 10, 1988. Evans was the floor general of Temple's first-ever No. 1-ranked team that same year.

TEMPLE'S FINAL FOUR TEAMS

arry Litwack was only in his fourth year as head coach at Temple when his 1955-56 team produced a sensational 27-4 record.

Harold "Hal" Lear and Guy Rodgers formed one of the best backcourts in the history of college basketball. "King" Lear scored a Temple single-season record 745 points that year, which still stands today. In his final game, a 90-81 victory over SMU for third place in that season's Final Four, Lear scored 48 points and was chosen the tournament's MVP. Rodgers was just a sophomore playing his first varsity season, but he tallied 573 points. Lear and Rodgers combined for 1,318 points.

The Owls' other starters were Hal "Hotsy" Reinfeld, Jay Norman, a 6-3 warrior who returned from military service, and Fred Cohen, a transfer from Duquesne, who pulled down an incredible 34 rebounds against Connecticut in the NCAA tournament. And believe it or not, that rebound total still remains as an NCAA tournament game mark.

Temple was eliminated by Iowa, 83-76, in an NCAA semifinal at Evanston, Illinois. San Francisco topped SMU in the other Final Four contest. Lear scored 48 points in a consolation game victory over SMU.

In 1957-58, Litwack had Temple back in the Final Four. Once again, the Owls grabbed third place by defeating Kansas State, 67-57, after having lost to Kentucky, 61-60, in an NCAA Final Four in Louis-

Harry Litwack presents Guy Rodgers with the MVP trophy and Jay Norman with the Most Inspirational trophy following Temple's 1957-58 season when it advanced to the Final Four and won its first outright Big 5 championship.

OBITUARIES

Angelo Musi, 91, basketball star

By Sally A. Downey
INQUIRER STAFF WRITER

Angelo Musi, 91, of Bryn Mawr, who captained the first professional basketball team in Philadelphia and went on to be a vending company executive, died Monday at home.

In 1946, Mr. Musi joined the Philadelphia Warriors in the new Basketball Association of America, now the NBA.

He described early Warriors games in the Arena in West Philadelphia in a 2003 WHYY TV12 documentary, *Philly Hoops*. After Ice Capades performances, the skating rink at the Arena was covered with a basketball floor, and moisture sweated all over it, Mr. Musi said. Warriors owner Eddie Gottlieb would put sawdust or oatmeal on the floor, but it didn't always work, Mr. Musi said. "Occasionally you'd dribble the ball and the ball wouldn't bounce back," he said. Gottlieb saw "6,400 people watching us. He was not about to give the money back."

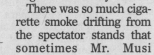

Angelo Musi

There was so much cigarette smoke drifting from the spectator stands that sometimes Mr. Musi couldn't see the basket, his son, Thomas, said. At 5-foot-9, "Ange was the smallest player on the team. He was a forward, not a guard, and he was the team's second-leading scorer," said Harvey Pollack, who was the Warriors assistant publicity director. In 1947 Mr. Musi led the Warriors to the first Basketball Association of America championship. He retired from the team in 1949.

Years later, he made fun of his small stature when he told Inquirer columnist Tom Fox: "If I suited up to try out for the 76ers today, Darryl Dawkins would die laughing. He'd probably pick me up and use me for a gusto dunk. It's not the same game I played when I was young."

In 2001 Sports Illustrated named Mr. Musi the third-best player for his height in NBA history.

Growing up in West Philadelphia, Mr. Musi spent hours shooting balls into a peach basket to be good enough to play with bigger boys. He was a star basketball player at Overbrook High School and the first of 12 Overbrook players to make it to the NBA. He also played soccer and was second baseman on the baseball team at Overbrook. After graduating, he spent a year at Brown Preparatory School in Philadelphia to qualify academically for a scholarship at Temple University.

At Temple, he captained the baseball and basketball teams. He was chosen for All-City basketball three times and All-Pennsylvania twice and earned honorable mention All-American in 1942, his senior year.

During World War II, he served in the Philippines and played baseball and basketball on Army teams.

After his discharge, he played a season with the Wilmington Bombers, an American Basketball League team.

When he left the Warriors, Mr. Musi went to work for Variety Vending Co. He eventually became vice president and regional manager of Macke Co., whose services included vending machines, employee cafeterias, and executive dining rooms. In a 1977 Inquirer interview, he estimated that his firm served 10 million snacks and meals a year. He retired in 1983.

An avid golfer, Mr. Musi was a longtime member of the Bala Golf Club, and he remained a basketball fan, Pollack said. Pollack is director of statistical information for the 76ers and publishes an annual NBA statistical yearbook. "Ange was always calling me with ideas about information to add," he said.

Mr. Musi was past president of Temple's Baseball, Basketball, and Varsity Clubs. He was a member of Temple's Athletics Hall of Fame and the Pennsylvania Sports Hall of Fame.

In addition to his son, Mr. Musi is survived by a daughter, Betty Ann Graham; four grandchildren; and nine great-grandchildren. His wife of 64 years, Lydia Villani Musi, died in 2006.

A Funeral Mass will be said at 10 a.m. tomorrow at St. Thomas of Villanova Chapel, 1229 Lancaster Ave. Rosemont. Burial will be in SS. Peter and Paul Cemetery, Marple Township.

Contact staff writer Sally A. Downey at 215-854-2913 or sdowney@phillynews.com.

The Warriors, Philadelphia's first professional basketball team, in 1947: (from left) Joe Fulks, George Senesky, Angelo Musi, Jerry Fleishman, and Johnny Murphy.

HOEVELER

VIRGINIA (nee James), 85, of Ocean City passed away Saturday, October 17, 2009 at Shore Memorial Hospital. She was a resident of Ocean City since 1982 and a member of St. Peter's United Methodist Church. Ginny was a Graduate of the University of Pennsylvania and a retired elementary teacher at Lynnewood School, Havertown, PA. Ginny loved her family, friends, a good conversation and chocolate. Ginny was predeceased by her husband, John and her children, John H. Hoeveler, MD. and Jill Hipkiss. She is survived by her sister, June Appleton of Ocean City; daughter-in-law, Carolyn Hoeveler of Somers Point; niece, Candace Appleton, of NY; grandchildren Christopher Hoeveler and wife Catherine of South Carolina and Jennifer Hipkiss of Pennsylvania and her great granddaughter, Alanna of South Carolina. Mrs. Hoeveler's Funeral service will be offered Friday, October 23, 2009 at 10:30 in the morning from St. Peters United Methodist Church, 8th Street at Central Avenue in Ocean City where friends may call from 9:30 until the time of service. Int. will follow in Arlington Cem., Drexel Hill, PA. Those who desire may send memorial contributions to St. Peter's United Methodist Church. To email condolences please visit godfreyfuneralhome.com

HURLEY

RITA P. (nee Blaser), Oct. 21, 2009, age 67 years. Beloved wife of the late Michael J.; devoted mother of Theresa Gribben (Christopher); loving grandmother of Megan; sister of Charles Blaser (Pat). Relatives and friends are invited to Viewing Friday, 6 to 8 P.M., and Saturday, 8:30 to 9:15 A.M., **HOLLEN FUNERAL HOME (Thomas J. Fluehr F.D.), 3160 Grant Ave. (W. of Academy Rd.).** Funeral Mass, 10 A.M., St. Anselm Church. Interment Resurrection Cemetery. Family prefers donations to American

KUENZEL

JULIUS ERIC, 72, of Jim Thorpe passed away on Tuesday October 20, 2009 at Lehigh Valley Hospital, Cedar Crest. He was the husband of Dora (Burnett) Kuenzel for 25 years. Born in Philadelphia he was the son of the late Julius & Janette (Elliott) Kuenzel. He was a graduate of Lasalle High School in Philadelphia & attended Drexel University majoring in engineering. He was in the Naval Air Reserves from 1955-65 stationed in Willow Grove. Julius worked for Local 420 steamfitters Union in Philadelphia & has been with Local 420 since 1957. He was a member of the Jim Thorpe Masonic Lodge and a 32 Degree Mason. Service: Memorial Service to be held Saturday October 24, 2009 at 1PM at S C H A E F F E R FUNERAL HOME 3rd & Alum Streets Lehighton, PA 18235.

LEONOWICZ

HENRIETTA JANE, October 13, 2009. Sister of John Leonowicz of Largo, Fla. Sadly missed by her niece and caregiver Kristine Lowe of Arnold, Md., 5 nephews, 3 nieces, 5 grand nephews, 6 grand nieces, 1 great grand nephew and 3 great grand nieces; daughter of the late John and Victoria (nee Banaszak). Relatives and friends invited to Viewing and Funeral Saturday 8:30 A.M. **TOMASZEWSKI FUNERAL HOME, 2728-30 E. Allegheny Ave...215-739-6624.** Funeral Mass 10:30 A.M. St. Adalbert Church. Int. Resurrection Cem.

LETHERLAND

JOHN H. SR. October 21, 2009 of Feasterville, Pa. Husband of Mary E. Father of John, Marie, Linda, Donna and Jeremiah; also surviving are 2 sisters, 13 grandchildren and 1 great granddaughter. Relative and friends are invited to attend his Funeral Mass, Saturday October 24, 2009 at 11:30 AM in Assumption B.V.M., Bristol Rd. and Meadowbrook Rd., Feasterville. Friends will be received after 10:30 AM until time of the Mass in the church.

MORITZ

HENRY T., age 90, of Rydal, died on October 21, 2009. He was the devoted husband of the late Helen M. Gutelius Moritz. He is survived by his loving children and their spouses, Gail M. and Andrew F. Oberta, Richard T. and Melinda C. Moritz and Joan L. and Dale F. Rutledge. Two grandchildren and three great grandchildren also survive him. Relatives and friends will be received on Friday, Oct. 23, 2009, from 10 to 11 A.M., **BARON ROWLAND FUNERAL HOME, 1059 Old York Rd., Abington,** where his Funeral Service will be held at 11 A.M. Burial will be in Hillside Cemetery. Memorial contributions may be sent to Abington Memorial Hospital Foundation Attn. Gribbel T.L.C. Fund, 1200 Old York Road, Abington PA 19001.

OSLICK

JANE (nee Hubbard), age 88, on October 20, 2009, of Lafayette Hill. Daughter of the late author Freeman Hubbard and singer Rachel (nee Buckner) Hubbard; sister of the late Eleanor Duncan; devoted wife of the late artist, Irvin Oslick. Survived by her brother, Roy Hubbard (Joan). Painter, swimmer, passionate Democrat and beloved mother of Alan Oslick (Yolanda), Judy Mo (Suchoon) and Melanie Kaneff; proud grandmother of Sage, Daisy and Clifton Mo, Elliot Loewenstein, Rachel Kaneff Parker, Jacob and Avram Oslick; great grandmother of Tallyn Mo, Julien and Grace Loewenstein; caring aunt to her nieces, nephews and their children. Graveside Service was held Wednesday, October 21st, at Northwood Cemetery. In lieu of flowers, memorials may be made to World Wildlife Fund, c/o www.worldwildlife.org
LOWNES F.H., Lafayette Hill

PFORTE

RUTH K., age 78, of Phila. on Oct. 19, 2009. Beloved wife of

SIPPEL

CELESTE A. (nee Szwanki), suddenly on October 17, 2009 at age 43. Wife of Joseph Sippel Jr. Devoted mother of Carly and Joseph III. Beloved daughter of Lorraine and the late Joseph Szwanki. Loving sister of Lori Scott (Timothy), and Joseph Szwanki (Cass). Also survived by many nieces, nephews, aunts, uncles. and cousins. Family will receive relatives and friends Saturday, 9 to 10 A.M., at St. Matthew Lower Church, 3000 Cottman Ave., Phila. PA 19149. Funeral Mass 10 A.M. Int. Northwood Cemetery. Donations in her memory to a charity of your choice appreciated.
LIVE...LAUGH...LOVE
Condolences to:
    www.meyersfh.com

SKIENDZIELEWSKI

THERESA L. "TREE" (nee Shinko), Monday, October 19, 2009, at the age of 55. Beloved wife of William McNamara; devoted mother of Lorraine Stieber (Thomas), Thomas Skiendzielewski (Danielle Quinn), Michele Siemenski (Walter), Robert McNamara, and Edward McNamara (Amy Davis); grandmother of Kylie and Keira; dear daughter of Nellie (nee Grivenski) Davis and the late Thomas Shinko; stepdaughter of Edwin Davis, Sr., sister of Carol Coney (Patrick), Edwin Davis, Jr. and Stephen Davis (Angelina). Relatives and friends are invited to Tree's Life Celebration Friday eve. 6-9 P.M. and Sat. morning 9-10 A.M. at the **JOHN F. GIVNISH OF ACADEMY RD., 10975 Academy Rd., Phila.** and to participate in her Funeral Mass 11 A.M. at Our Lady of Good Council Church. Interment private. In lieu of flowers donations to the American Cancer Society, 1626 Locust St. Phila. PA 19103 would be appreciated by the family.
    1-877-GIVNISH
    www.lifecelebration.com

SNITYNSKI

ANASTASIA "Nancy", Age 94,

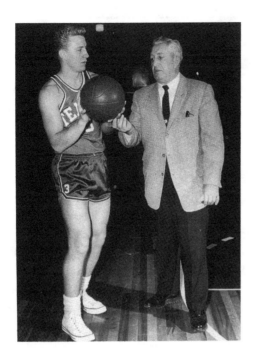

Bill "Pickles" Kennedy was Guy Rodgers' backcourt mate for one year, helping Harry Litwack's Owls to the 1958 Final Four. Kennedy then took over the playmaking and scoring load for his final two seasons. He was named All-America in both basketball and baseball.

ville. The Owls lost just three games that season and two were to national champion Kentucky. The Owl starters were Rodgers, Norman, Elmer (Tink) Van Patton, Mel Brodsky, and Bill (Pickles) Kennedy.

Temple won 27 games that year with an impressive 25-game winning streak. This team was certainly one of the best in Temple basketball history. Rodgers, a key member of that team, was a consensus first team All-American along with Oscar Robertson, Wilt Chamberlain, Elgin Baylor, and Don Hennon. Rodgers scored 603 points that season to finish his career with 1,767 points. He currently ranks third on the Owls' all-time scoring list.

Seniors Norman and Van Patton were drafted by the Philadelphia Warriors, as was Rodgers. Norman scored 1,024 points and finished his career with 917 rebounds.

Lear and Norman remained Temple teammates in the Eastern Basketball League. Norman became a terrific big man for Litwack, Don Casey, and Chaney.

Harry Litwack is the only Temple basketball coach or player to be inducted into the Naismith Hall of Fame.

Harry "The Chief" Litwack's remarkable run as a Temple player, assistant coach and head coach spanned six decades. It included 373 victories, two Final Fours, an NIT championship and an induction into the Naismith Memorial Basketball Hall of Fame.

TEMPLE'S 1969
NIT CHAMPIONSHIP TEAM

When you think about championship teams at Temple, the school's 1969 NIT champions come to mind. The last team invited to the NIT, the Owls capped a series of upsets by hammering Boston College in the championship game. BC tried hard to win; the Eagles wanted to send Bob Cousy, who was coaching his last game, home a winner.

In the first round, Eddie Mast's 20 points led the Owls to a 82-66 victory over Florida. John Baum scored 31 points and took 23 rebounds in a 94-78 win over St. Peter's on St. Patrick's Day.

In the next game, Temple bounced Tennessee, 65-58. A late 14-3 explosion helped the Owls crush Boston College, 89-76 in the NIT championship game. Baum, Mast, Joe Cromer, and Tony Brocchi never came off the floor in the tournament. Bill Strunk left the championship game on a tender ankle, and Tom Wieczerak provided key baskets. BC's Terry Driscoll was named MVP—writers voted while the Eagles were ahead—but Baum accepted the championship. "This is the happiest day of my coaching life," said Harry Litwack, Temple head coach. The Owls finished the season 22-8.

The 1968-69 NIT Champion Temple University Basketball Team

Sitting right to left: Gavin White, assistant director of athletics Gordon Mulava, Joe Cromer, captain John Baum, coach Harry Litwack, Jim Snook, Eddie Mast, Carl Brooks, director of athletics Ernie Casale. Standing left to right: sports information director Al Shrier, trainer Ted Quedenfeld, assistant coach Don Casey, Tony Brocchi, Tom Wieczerak, John Richardson, Pat Cassidy, Bill Strunk, assistant coach Jay Norman, assistant coach Jim Wilson, manager Mel Greenberg.

PENN'S '79 TEAM ADVANCES TO THE FINAL FOUR

Penn's 1979 team was one of the most talented teams in the history of the Ivy League. Under head coach Bob Weinhauer, the Quakers won four times in Raleigh, North Carolina to reach the NCAA Final Four.

Penn slipped by Iona (73-69) and then Tim Smith carried the Quakers past North Carolina (72-71) before a large Tar Heel crowd in Raleigh. Tony Price and Matt White then led Penn by Syracuse (84-76) and St. John's (64-62) in Greensboro.

Penn lost 101-67 to eventual champion Michigan State, led by Magic Johnson and Greg Kelser. The Quakers lost third (96-93) in triple overtime to DePaul, led by Mark Aguirre. Price was the tournament's top scorer with 142 points, more than Johnson and Indiana State's Larry Bird. Penn's starters were Price, White, Smith, James Salters, and Bobby Willis. The Quakers finished the season 25-7. They were also Big 5 champions.

This team was so good, it embarrassed many Ivy people, who demanded restrictions that would make an Ivy Final Four unlikely.

1978-79 Pennsylvania Basketball Team

Front row, left to right: Ed Kuhl, Bobby Willis, Tony Price, Matt White, Tim Smith. Second row, left to right, coach Bob Weinhauer, manager Kevin O'Brien, Tom Condon, Vincent Ross, Tom Leifsen, Ted Flick, assistant coach Bob Staak. Standing left to right: assistant coach Dennis Jackson, Angelo Reynolds, James Salters, David Jackson, Ken Hall, manager Pete Bagatta.

PENN'S '71 TEAM FINISHES THE REGULAR SEASON WITH AN UNDEFEATED RECORD

The Penn Quakers put together an incredible 28-0 regular season, outscoring their opponents by nearly 17 points a game. Since then, only nine teams have managed to go through the regular season unbeaten: UCLA '72 and '73; North Carolina State '73; Indiana '75 and '76; Rutgers '76; Indiana State '79; Alcorn State '79, and UNLV '91.

Villanova crushed Penn, 90-47, in the NCAA tournament at North Carolina. The Quakers, under head coach Dick Harter, had outstanding players such as Bob Morse, Corky Calhoun, Dave Wohl, and Steve Bilsky. Penn's top scorers were Bob Morse (15.4 ppg) and Dave Wohl (15.3 ppg).

The Quakers, 4-0 in the Big 5, finished 28-1. Bilsky is now Penn's athletic director after serving as AD at George Washington. Morse had a great career in Italy. Wohl is the vice president of basketball operations for the Miami Heat. Calhoun played for Portland's NBA title team.

1970-71 Pennsylvania Basketball Team, Big 5 Champions.

First Row, left to right: Coach Dick Harter, Jim Wolf, Jim Haney, Steve Bilsky, Dave Wohl, John Koller, assistant coach Ray Edelman. Second row, left to right, trainer Bob Matthews, Keith Hansen, Corky Calhoun, Bob Morse, Phil Hankinson, Craig Littlepage, manager Eddie Spiegel. Third row, left to right, Bill Walters, Alan Cotler, Steve Batory, Ron Billingslea.

ST. JOSEPH'S CAPTURES THE FIRST BIG 5 CHAMPIONSHIP IN 1955-56

S t. Joseph's has played a key role in Big 5 basketball. The 1955-56 Hawks team under head coach Dr. Jack Ramsay won the first Big 5 championship. St. Joseph's compiled an overall 23-6 record that year.

"I would have to say winning the first Big 5 title was something very special," Ramsay said. "That first year, we had some fine players like Billy Lynch, Al Juliana, and Mike Fallon. We didn't have a lot of size, but these guys played very well together."

Lynch, along with St. Joseph's teammates Juliana, Fallon, and Kurt Engelbert received first-team All Big 5 honors. In the 1950s, St. Joseph's and Temple dominated the Big 5. The Hawks were 14-2 in Big 5 games in the '50s with two outright titles and one shared.

St. Joseph's posted a 4-0 record en route to its first Big 5 championship.

ST. JOSEPH'S 1955-56 RESULTS

(Won 23, Lost 6; Big 5: 4-0)

Date	SJU	OPP	
12/1	89	Fordham	71
12/3	84	Rhode Island	72
12/6	76	Millersville	60
12/9	60	George Washington	71
12/12	96	Pennsylvania Military	53
12/14	83	Villanova	70
12/16	66	Connecticut	71
12/20	83	Albright	81
1/4	69	La Salle	56
1/7	76	Muhlenberg	71
1/10	98	Elizabethtown	65
1/13	75	Manhattan	74
1/18	83	Drexel	57
1/25	74	West Chester	60
1/28	72	Pennsylvania	60
2/1	72	Georgetown	84
2/3	68	Lafayette	79
2/11	84	Furman	82
2/15	77	Franklin & Marshall	51
2/18	80	St. Francis-NY	76
2/22	77	Temple	68
2/25	72	Virginia	69
2/29	74	Muhlenberg	63
3/3	91	Delaware	77
3/6	84	Lafayette	80
3/10	82	Temple	89
3/20	74	Seton Hall	65
3/22	79	Louisville	89
3/24	93	St. Francis-NY	82

ST. JOSEPH'S UPSETS NO. 1-RANKED DePAUL IN NCAA TOURNEY

O n March 14, 1981, St. Joseph's pulled one of the biggest upsets in NCAA tournament his-tory, beating No. 1 DePaul 49-48 on John Smith's buzzer beater layup. After DePaul missed a free throw, Bryan Warrick dribbled through the Blue Demons and passed to the right corner to Lonnie McFarlan who fed Smith. A stunned Mark Aguirre, in his final college game, walked two miles back to his Dayton hotel in shock. Jimmy Lynam's 1981 Hawks (25-8) also defeated Creighton (59-57) and Boston College (42-41) before losing (78-46) to NCAA champion Indiana, led by Isiah Thomas.

The Hawks' key players were Smith, Warrick, Jeffery Clark, McFarlan, and Tony Costner. "It was a great win for our program," Clark said. "The win over DePaul put St. Joseph's on the map. DePaul

St. Joseph's Jeffery Clark displays his shooting form during a game at the Palestra. *Photo by Ed Mahan.*

had all the superstars. They were on national tele-vision all the time. We were just trying to get some recognition. As it turned out, it was a big win for us." The oft-shown celebration featured Lynam dancing onto the court and then hugging his daughter, Dee.

St. Joseph's Bryan Warrick (13) passes the ball during a classic St.Joseph's -Villanova game. Also pictured is Villanova's Alex Bradley. *Photo by Ed Mahan.*

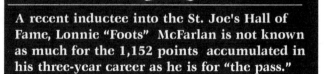

A recent inductee into the St. Joe's Hall of Fame, Lonnie "Foots" McFarlan is not known as much for the 1,152 points accumulated in his three-year career as he is for "the pass."

ST. JOSEPH'S PLACES THIRD IN NCAA TOURNAMENT PLAY

St. Joseph's has produced some fine teams over the years. However, Jack Ramsay, the Hawks' head coach, had his most successful team in 1961. That year, St. Joseph's (25-5) won the Big 5 City Series and scored a lot of points along the way.

The highest scoring game in NCAA tournament history, prior to the Bo Kimble-led Loyola Marymount team, was the four-overtime 127-120 St. Joseph's win over Utah. Jack Egan led the Hawks with 42 points while Jim Lynam added 31. In all, six Hawks scored in double figures.

St. Joseph's other tournament victories were over Princeton (72-67) and Wake Forest (96-86) in Charlotte, North Carolina and Utah in Kansas City, Missouri. St. Joseph's only loss in the tournament was to Ohio State, 95-69.

St. Joseph's third-place finish in the tournament would eventually be vacated by the NCAA. Nevertheless, the Hawks had a marvelous year. Egan set records with 636 points in a season and 47 in a game. He scored 47 as St. Joseph's beat Gettysburg, 85-76. The Hawks also set a school record by winning 15 straight games late in the season, a mark that still stands.

Ramsay guided SJU to 234 wins, ten postseason tournaments, seven Philadelphia Big 5 titles and the school's only NCAA Final Four appearance, 1960-61.

St. Joseph's legendary Jack Ramsay put the Hawks on the national basketball map during an eleven-year stint from 1955-56 through 1965-66.

LA SALLE POSTS 30-WIN SEASON AS LIONEL SIMMONS NAMED PLAYER OF THE YEAR

Lionel Simmons was elected 1990 National Player of the Year after leading the Explorers to a sensational 30-2 record. Simmons scored 3,217 career points with the Explorers, but he isn't the Big 5's top scorer. Mark Macon of Temple is, with 347 points. La Salle's Michael Brooks had 344 points, while Simmons finished with 301.

Simmons helped the Explorers win their last 21 regular season games in 1990 and beat Southern Mississippi in the NCAA first round. That is the Big 5's only 20-game winning streak since 1978.

In 1989-90, La Salle surrounded Simmons with such great players as Doug Overton, Randy Woods, Jack Hurd, and super sub Bobby Johnson. In addition to winning the Big 5 title, the Explorers also won the Metro Atlantic Athletic Conference regular season and tournament championships. La Salle's two losses were to Loyola Marymount, featuring Bo Kimble and Hank Gathers, and Clemson in the NCAA tournament.

1990 National Player of the Year Lionel Simmons.

In 1990, Lionel Simmons was the Explorers' leading scorer with a 26.5 average. Simmons was one of the top scorers in college basketball.

LA SALLE's 23-1 TEAM UNABLE TO GO TO THE TOURNAMENT BECAUSE OF PROBATION

La Salle, coached by Naismith Basketball Hall of Famer Tom Gola, posted a 23-1 record and finished No. 2 in the polls behind UCLA in 1969, but could not go to the NCAA tournament because the school was on probation. The Explorers had some tremendous players such as Ken Durrett, Larry Cannon, Roland Taylor, Bernie Williams, Stan Wlodarczyk, and Ed Chesney.

The Explorers were known for their devastating fastbreak. They had one of the best ball movement teams in college basketball. La Salle defeated Indiana, Creighton, Western Kentucky, and Detroit. The Explorers' only loss was to South Carolina in the Quaker City Tournament.

Durrett and Howard Porter shared the Geasey Award as Big 5 MVPs. Durrett and Cannon made first team All-Big 5.

La Salle Assistant Coach Ken Durrett shared the Big 5 MVP award in 1969.

LA SALLE's 1968-69 RECORD AGAINST BIG 5 OPPONENTS

OPPONENT	LSC	OPP
Pennsylvania	78	64
Temple	101	85
Villanova	74	67
St. Joseph's	84	67

South Carolina was the only team to defeat La Salle during the 1968-69 season. The Gamecocks edged the Explorers 62-59 in the Quaker City Tournament at the Palestra.

THE BIG 5'S GREATEST PLAYERS

The *Philadelphia Daily News* in cooperation with the Big 5 and former executive director Dan Baker sifted through more than 4,500 pieces of mail to determine a *Daily News* all-time Big 5 team. The *Daily News* ran ballots for 10 days and readers sent in their Big 5 "Dream Team." Here are the top 20 finishers in the voting by *Daily News* readers. A team of *Daily News* sportswriters and sports editors then selected a top 10 from this list, indicated in boldface below.

ALL-TIME BIG 5 DREAM TEAM

1. **Lionel Simmons, La Salle**
2. **Guy Rodgers, Temple**
3. **Ken Durrett, La Salle**
4. **Howard Porter, Villanova**
5. **Wali Jones, Villanova**
6. **Ed Pinckney, Villanova**
7. **Mark Macon, Temple**
8. **Cliff Anderson, St. Joseph's**
9. **Corky Calhoun, Penn**
10. **Michael Brooks, La Salle**
11. Mike Bantom, St. Joseph's
12. Eddie Jones, Temple
13. Matt Guokas, St. Joseph's
14. Hal Lear, Temple
15. Larry Cannon, La Salle
16. Tim Perry, Temple
17. Dave Wohl, Penn
18. Joe Bryant, La Salle
19. Aaron McKie, Temple
20. Nate Blackwell, Temple

LIONEL SIMMONS

Lionel Simmons, also known as "Train," finished his career at La Salle as the third leading scorer in NCAA history with 3,217 points, trailing only Pete Maravich (3,667) and Freeman Williams (3,249). Simmons was the only player in NCAA history to score over 3,000 points and grab over 1,000 rebounds. In 1989-90, he captained the Explorers, who set a single-season La Salle record with 30 victories and whose 32-2 record was the best in Division I. He was a consensus first-team All-America and winner of the John Wooden Award as well as receiving Player of the Year honors from the Naismith Hall of Fame, Eastman Kodak, Associated Press, United Press International and the United Basketball Writers Association. He also won three consecutive Robert Geasey Awards as the Big 5 Player of the Year.

Year	G	Pts.	Reb.
1986-87	33	20.3	9.8
1989-88	34	23.3	11.4
1988-89	32	28.4	11.4
1989-90	32	26.5	11.1
Career	131	24.6	10.9

Simmons, a 6-7, 210-pound forward, was selected by the Sacramento Kings with the seventh overall pick in the NBA draft. In his first season with the Kings, he finished second in the balloting to Derrick Coleman for Rookie of the Year. The former Explorer has been a solid performer for Sacramento during his six-year career averaging 17.0 points, 7.9 rebounds and 4.2 assists a game.

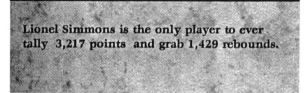

Lionel Simmons is the only player to ever tally 3,217 points and grab 1,429 rebounds.

Train, recruited by Lefty Ervin and signed by Speedy Morris, was the Explorers' mainstay from day one. Simmons played his scholastic basketball at South Philadelphia High School. In 1987, he led the Rams to the Philadelphia Public League championship.

"I was very fortunate to get Lionel Simmons," Morris said. "He was one of the best high school players in the country."

GUY RODGERS

When you talk about the greatest Big 5 ballhandlers, Guy Rodgers has to be near the top of the list. Rodgers thrilled fans with his terrific ballhandling, passing and scoring. Rodgers played with the great Hal Lear at Temple to form one of the greatest backcourts in college basketball history.

In 1955-56, he led the Owls to a 27-4 record and to the NCAA Final Four. The following year, he averaged 20.4 while leading Temple to a 20-9 record and to a third-place finish in the NIT. In his senior year, he averaged 20.1 as Temple posted a 27-3 mark and placed third in the NCAA tournament. He helped the Owls capture the 1958 Big 5 championship. He won three consecutive MVP honors in the Big 5. He also won the Big 5's Food Fair sportsmanship trophy.

Rodgers, a 6-0, 185-pound guard, played 12 years in the NBA for the Philadelphia Warriors, San Francisco Warriors, Chicago Bulls, Cincinnati Royals and the Milwaukee Bucks. He scored 10,415 points and dished out 6,917 assists.

Retired in Los Angeles, Rodgers often visits his protege, Sonny Hill. In a recent summer visit to McGonigle Hall, Rodgers performed his old nickel trick, smacking a coin off a friend's palm before the person could close his hand.

Guy Rodgers is fourth on the all-time scoring list at Temple University with 1,767 points.

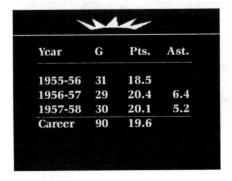

Year	G	Pts.	Ast.
1955-56	31	18.5	
1956-57	29	20.4	6.4
1957-58	30	20.1	5.2
Career	90	19.6	

KEN DURRETT

Ken Durrett had some classic matchups with Villanova's Howard Porter. The La Salle - Villanova rivalry during the late 60s and early 70s kept The Palestra rocking.

"To have someone playing in the same city at that competitive level was such a thrill to me," Porter said in an interview with *Daily News* sportswriter Dick Jerardi. "Just to have an opportunity to play against a guy with that kind of skill really helped to bring my game out."

In 1969, Durrett, along with teammates Larry Cannon, Bernie Williams and Roland Taylor, were ranked No. 2 in the country behind UCLA. However, La Salle (23-1) was on probation and unable to compete in the NCAA tournament.

Durrett, a multi-talented player who could go inside as well as out-side, led the Explorers in scoring and rebounding in each of his three seasons. He won two outright Geasey Awards (1970 and '71) and shared one with Porter (1969) as the Big 5's Most Valuable Player.

Unfortunately, Durrett, a 6-7, 190-pound forward, tore his anterior cruciate knee ligament his senior year. This injury limited his play in the pros. He played only four years in the NBA with the Cincinnati Royals, Kansas City Omaha Kings and the Philadelphia 76ers.

Durrett has a sporting goods business in Pittsburgh.

La Salle's Ken Durrett captured three straight Big 5 Player of the Year Awards in 1969, 1970, and 1971.

Year	G	Pts.	Reb.
1968-69	24	20.0	11.8
1969-70	26	24.3	12.1
1970-71	21	27.0	12.0
Career	71	23.7	12.0

HOWARD PORTER

H oward (Geezer) Porter holds the Big 5 record for most points in an NCAA tournament with 217. Porter was well known for his battles with Durrett in City Series games. He and Durrett shared Big 5 MVP honors in 1969 as sophomores. Porter received first-team All-Big 5 honors three consecutive years. However, he will always be remembered for his brilliant play in the NCAA Finals against UCLA. Porter outplayed All-Americans Sidney Wicks and Curtis Rowe. But UCLA edged Villanova 68-62, to capture another national title.

Year	G	Pts.	Reb.
1968-69	30	22.4	12.5
1969-70	29	22.2	15.1
1970-71	29	23.5	14.9
Career	88	23.0	15.0

Howard Porter holds the Villanova record for most rebounds in a game with 30 against St. Peter's in a 1971 game.

Porter finished his career as the school's second-leading scorer (2,026 points). He is currently fourth on the list. He holds the Villanova record for rebounds in a game (30), season (503 in 1970-71) and career (1,317). He is also a member of the Big 5 Hall of Fame.

Porter, a 6-8, 220-pound forward, played seven NBA seasons with the Chicago Bulls, New York Knicks, Detroit Pistons and the New Jersey Nets.

WALI JONES

Wali Jones was one of the best guards to ever play in the Big 5. Jones, a 6-2, 180-pound guard, shared two Geasey Awards as Big 5 MVP (1963 and 64) with Jim Lynam and Steve Courtin respectively. He was named to the NCAA tournament's All-East Region team as the Wildcats won two games, defeating Providence and Princeton. Jones also received All-Big 5 honors each season at Villanova.

He finished his career as the school's fifth-leading scorer with 1,428 points. The former Overbrook High star is an original member of the Big 5 Hall of Fame.

Jones played 10 seasons in the NBA with the Baltimore Bullets, Philadelphia 76ers, Milwaukee Bucks and Detroit Pistons. Jones was the starting guard 1966-67 Philadelphia 76ers team that won the NBA championship. That team, which started Jones, Hal Greer, Wilt Chamberlain, Luke Jackson and Chet Walker was voted the best team in the history of the NBA. Jones played one ABA season with the Utah Stars.

He currently works for the Miami Heat as Vice President of community relations. Jones' primary responsibilities are to work with the Miami Heat Community Foundation and other South Florida agencies to establish a positive relationship between the team and its community. Jones was promoted to Vice President in 1991 after spending the previous two years as Director of Community Relations.

Year	G	Pts.	Ast.
1961-62	28	17.1	
1962-63	29	16.7	
1963-64	28	16.4	
Career	85	16.8	2.7

Villanova's Wali Jones was the first multiple winner of the Geasey MVP Award since Guy Rodgers and the last until Ken Durrett.

ED PINCKNEY

E d Pinckney was named MVP of the 1985 NCAA tournament after Villanova's stunning victory over Georgetown. He topped the Wildcats in blocks, rebounds and field goal percentage in each of his four seasons. Pinckney is Villanova's all-time leader in field goal percentage at .605, fourth in rebounds (1,107) and fifth in scoring (1,865 points). He was named MVP of the Big 5 in 1985. In 1985, he was a first-round draft pick of the Phoenix Suns. He spent two years with the Suns before they traded him to the Sacramento Kings. After two years with the Kings, he was sent to the Boston Celtics. His best year with the Celtics was the 1991-92 season, when he averaged 7.6 points. A year ago, he was traded to the Milwaukee Bucks.

Pinckney recently completed his tenth season in the NBA. Last season, Pinckney played half a season with the NBA expansion team the Toronto Raptors before being traded to the Philadelphia 76ers.

Playing in the Sonny Hill League and Sonny Hill College League, Easy Ed said he was tired of hearing New York jokes. He also participated in a few Charles Baker League (Philadelphia summer basketball league for the pros) all-star games.

"I really had a great time playing in the Sonny Hill League," Pinckney said. "It gave me an opportunity to play against a lot of Big 5 players during the summer. That's where the rivalry starts. You play against your friends in the summer, then again in the winter."

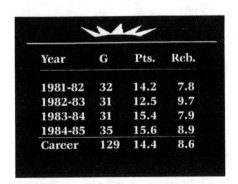

Year	G	Pts.	Reb.
1981-82	32	14.2	7.8
1982-83	31	12.5	9.7
1983-84	31	15.4	7.9
1984-85	35	15.6	8.9
Career	129	14.4	8.6

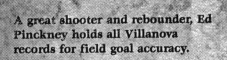

A great shooter and rebounder, Ed Pinckney holds all Villanova records for field goal accuracy.

MARK MACON

ark Macon was a huge star for John Chaney and the Temple Owls. Macon was the nation's leading freshman scorer (20.6) while helping the Owls to a 32-2 record and the No. 1 ranking in the polls. Macon, a 6-5, 185-pound guard, left Temple as the school's all-time leader in scoring (2,609 points) and steals (281). He led the Owls to the NCAA Final Eight twice in his four years. He was named the outstanding player at NCAA Eastern Regionals in 1991. He was selected as the Big 5's MVP his senior year. Macon, a McDonald's high school All-American, was one of the most talented players to ever play in the Big 5.

As a freshman, Macon got Howard Evans to teach him the entire Temple system and John Chaney's parables before October 15 start of practice.

Macon was drafted by the Denver Nuggets with the eighth pick in the first round. He played two seasons with the Nuggets and the start of the third before coming to the Detroit Pistons with Marcus Liberty in trade for Alvin Robertson. Macon just finished his fifth NBA season. He was released by the Pistons this year. But throughout his pro career, he's been known for his tenacious defense.

The Temple Owls won 94 times during Mark Macon's college career and were ranked #1 in the nation during his freshman season.

Year	G	Pts.	Reb.
1987-88	34	20.6	5.7
1988-89	30	18.3	5.6
1989-90	31	21.9	
1990-91	31	22.0	4.9
Career	126	20.7	x

CLIFF ANDERSON

Cliff Anderson scored a single-season record 116 points in Big 5 games for an amazing 26.5 point a game average. Anderson, St. Joseph's 6-4, 200-pound forward, holds school records for highest single-season scoring average (26.5 in 1966-67), highest single-season rebounding average (15.5 in 1964-65) and career rebounds. He scored 1,728 points in his career. He is currently fourth on the Hawks' all-time scoring list. As a senior, he led the Hawks with a 66-18 record and two Big 5 titles.

In 1967, he won the Geasey Award as Big 5 MVP. Anderson, an original member of the Big 5 Hall of Fame, played in the NBA for three season with the Los Angeles Lakers, Cleveland Cavaliers and the Philadelphia 76ers. He also played in the ABA for one year with the Denver Nuggets.

Anderson is currently working in private industry.

Year	G	Pts.	Ast.
1964-65	29	17.9	15.5
1965-66	29	17.9	14.0
1966-67	26	26.5	14.3
Career	84	20.6	14.6

Cliff Anderson led St. Joseph's in scoring and rebounding in each of his three seasons, and his 15.5 rebound average as a sophomore is still a school record.

CORKY CALHOUN

Corky Calhoun was one of the most versatile players to ever play in the Big 5. Calhoun, a 6-7, 210-pound forward, could also play guard for the Quakers. In 1972, he shared the Geasey Award as Big 5 MVP with Villanova's Chris Ford.

He finished his career as the 11th leading scorer in school history (1,066 points). Calhoun played on three consecutive NCAA tourney teams at Penn. He played for head coaches Dick Harter and Chuck Daly. In 1976, he was inducted into the Big 5 Hall of Fame.

Calhoun played in the NBA for eight seasons with the Phoenix Suns, Los Angeles Lakers, Portland Trail Blazers and the Indiana Pacers. He was a member of the 1977 Trail Blazer team that won the NBA championship. The Trail Blazers were coached by ex-St. Joseph's coaches Jack Ramsay and Jack McKinney.

He was best known for his defense. In the NBA, he played the other team's top scorer. Calhoun always had his work cut out for him, but never seemed to complain.

A two-time MVP, Corky Calhoun was the team's most complete player when the Quakers went 78-6 and were ranked second and third in the nation his last two seasons.

Year	G	Pts.	Reb.
1969-70	27	14.6	8.9
1970-71	29	10.1	8.6
1971-72	28	13.5	6.9
Career	84	12.7	8.1

MICHAEL BROOKS

Michael Brooks, a consensus All-American, was named Player of the Year by the National Association of Basketball Coaches. Brooks, a 6-7, 220-pound forward, is second on La Salle's career scoring list with 2,628 points. A spectacular combination of strength and grace highlighted Brooks' play as did his intelligence on the court.

Brooks played his high school basketball at West Catholic. He received All-Catholic League and All-City honors. He also participated in the Sonny Hill League.

He was named captain of the 1980 U.S. Olympic team (which eventually boycotted the Moscow Games). He led his team in rebounding each of his four seasons. Brooks scored a school-record 51 points in a triple overtime loss at Brigham Young on December 15, 1979. Able to outspeed rival big men, Brooks made "The System" work for Paul Westhead.

In 1980, he was a first-round draft pick of the San Diego Clippers. Brooks played four years for the Clippers. He also played one season with the Indiana Pacers and Denver Nuggets. He is currently playing professional basketball in France.

A prolific scorer, La Salle's Michael Brooks graduated as the school's all-time top scorer and was seventh on the NCAA's all-time list.

Year	G	Pts.	Reb.
1976-77	29	20.0	14.1
1977-78	28	24.9	2.8
1978-79	26	23.3	13.4
1979-80	31	24.1	11.5
Career	114	23.1	12.8

MIKE BANTOM

Mike Bantom was a two-time All-Big 5 selection at St. Joseph's. Bantom, a 6-9, 200-pound forward, played on the 1972 U.S. Olympic team. He was known for his strong inside scoring, rebounding and defense. Bantom is just one of four Hawk players to compile over 1,000 points and rebounds in a career. He still ranks seventh on St. Joseph's all-time scoring list with 1,684 points and second on the rebound chart with 1,151 caroms. Bantom received All-Big 5 honors his junior and senior years. He led the Hawks to postseason appearances in the NCAA and NIT.

Bantom played nine seasons in the NBA with the Phoenix Suns, Seattle SuperSonics, New York Knicks, Indiana Pacers and the Philadelphia 76ers. In 1981-82, he helped the Sixers defeat the Boston Celtics and get to the NBA finals. Bantom was recognized as one of the league's toughest defenders.

He now represents the NBA in international business. He gained contacts and expertise during the years he played in Italy.

St. Joseph's Mike Bantom is second on the team's all-time rebounding list (1,151). Until Carlin Warley did it in 1994, Bantom had been the last player to average double figures in rebounding for a season.

Year	G	Pts.	Reb.
1976-77	29	20.0	14.1
1977-78	28	24.9	2.8
1978-79	26	23.3	13.4
1979-80	31	24.1	11.5
Career	114	23.1	12.8

EDDIE JONES

Eddie Jones, a first-round pick of the Los Angeles Lakers, averaged 19.2 points, 6.8 rebounds, 2.3 steals and 1.5 blocked shots for Temple his senior year. Jones, a 6-6, 190-pound forward, was also the Atlantic 10 Conference Player of the Year.

He led the Owls to three consecutive NCAA tournament appearances. In 1992-93, Jones exploded onto the national scene with tremendous performances in the NCAA tournament. The Owls' high-flying swingman helped Temple to advance to the NCAA's Elite Eight. He teamed up with Aaron McKie, a first-round pick of the Portland Trail Blazers, to form one of the best combinations in college basketball. McKie and Jones are two of the best players to ever play for John Chaney.

"I really enjoyed playing ball with Eddie," McKie said. "We developed a great friendship during our playing days at Temple. We still stay in touch with each other. Last summer, we spent a lot of time playing basketball in Philly."

This past season, Jones played a key role in guiding the Lakers to the first round of the NBA playoffs. Two years ago, he was named MVP of the NBA's Rookie All-Star Game.

"Eddie has the potential to be a terrific player in this league," said Del Harris, Lakers head coach. "We're very pleased with him. He can shoot, take the ball to the basket, run the floor and play excellent defense. Moreover, he was well coached by John Chaney."

Eddie Jones, Aaron McKie, and Rick Brunson carried Temple to the NCAA Final Eight in 1993.

Year	G	Pts.	Reb.
1991-92	29	11.5	4.1
1992-93	32	17.0	7.0
1993-94	31	19.2	6.8
Career	92	16.0	6.0

MATT GUOKAS

Matt Guokas, a two-time All-Big 5 selection, played for Jack Ramsay at St. Joseph's. Guokas led the Hawks to back to back Big 5 titles and appearances in the NCAA tournament. He played one year at the University of Miami before transferring to St. Joseph's. He played with Clifford Anderson, Tom Duff, Billy Oakes and Marty Ford on the Hawks' 1965-66 team that averaged 91.1 points a game. Guokas is a member of the Big 5 Hall of Fame.

Guokas, a 6-5, 185-pound guard, played for the Philadelphia 76ers, Chicago Bulls, Cincinnati Royals, Kansas City Omaha Kings, Houston Rockets and Buffalo Braves. However, the highlight of his pro career was playing on the 1966-67 Philadelphia 76ers NBA championship team, which featured Wilt Chamberlain, Billy Cunningham, Wali Jones, Hal Greer, Chet Walker and Luke Jackson.

Guokas is currently a color commentator for the NBA games on NBC-TV. Matt Guokas Sr., his dad, was the big man of St. Joseph's popular "Mighty Mites." Matt Guokas III played center for the Hawks after starring for Speedy Morris at Penn Charter.

Matt Guokas Jr. is the middle man in three generations of Matt Guokases to play at St. Joseph's.

Year	G	Pts.	Reb.
1964-65	29	13.3	5.3
1965-66	29	17.5	6.1
Career	58	15.4	5.7

HAL LEAR

Hal Lear, one of the best jumpshooters in the history of the Big 5, teamed up at Temple with Guy Rodgers as one of the best backcourt tandems in the 1950s. Lear scored a career total of 1,472 points. The Owls' 6-3 guard scored 745 points in one season, which is still a school record today. Lear scored 160 points in five NCAA tournament games in 1956 as the Owls advanced to the Final Four. Only four players have surpassed that mark: Glen Rice (Michigan '89: 183); Bill Bradley (Princeton '65: 177); Elvin Hayes (Houston '68: 167); and Danny Manning (Kansas '88: 163). He scored 48 points in his final game as Temple defeated Southern Methodist, 90-81 for third place in the NCAA tournament; he was named MVP after that game.

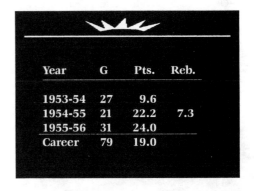

Year	G	Pts.	Reb.
1953-54	27	9.6	
1954-55	21	22.2	7.3
1955-56	31	24.0	
Career	79	19.0	

Lear was such a confident shooter, he won contests in which he would count his shot if it touched the rim before dropping through the net. He received first team All-Big 5 honors in 1956.

Lear is a member of the Big 5 Hall of Fame. After his college career, he played in the old Eastern League. He also played in the Charles Baker League.

Temple's Hal Lear scored a record 745 points as a senior, and had a remarkable run in the NCAAs.

LARRY CANNON

L arry Cannon was a key member of La Salle's 23-1 team in 1968-69. Cannon, a 6-5, 195-pound forward, was a big part of the Explorers' devastating fastbreak triggered by the rebounding of Ken Durrett, ballhandling of Roland Taylor and the jumpshooting of Bernie Williams. He received first team All-Big 5 honors in 1968 and 69.

Cannon, an original member of the Big 5 Hall of Fame, finished his career as the fourth-leading scorer in school history with 1,430 points. He is currently No. 15 on the all-time scoring list.

Cannon played four seasons in the American Basketball Association (ABA) with the Miami Floridians, Denver Nuggets, Memphis Pros and Indiana Pacers. He also played one season with the Philadelphia 76ers.

Year	G	Pts.	Ast.
1966-67	24	18.7	2.9
1967-68	28	19.5	4.8
1968-69	23	18.9	5.8
Career	75	19.1	4.6

La Salle's Larry Cannon played three seasons for the Explorers and had three different coaches. The one thing that remained consistent was Cannon's ability to score.

TIM PERRY

Tim Perry was named the Atlantic 10 Conference Player of the Year in 1987-88. Perry, a 6-9, 220-pound forward, led Temple to a No. 1 ranking with a 32-2 record. He averaged 14.5 points and eight rebounds his senior year. In 1988, he was named the Atlantic 10 Player of the Year, and he received first-team All-Big 5 honors. Perry credits Temple coach John Chaney for his success.

"Coach Chaney gave me a lot of confidence," Perry said. "He drilled me on the fundamentals. He inspired me to work extremely hard on my game. He also taught me a lot about life. You know, coach Chaney is not just a basketball coach, he's a teacher too."

Perry finished his college career as the Owls' all-time leading shotblocker (392) and fourth all-time leading rebounder (985). He was named MVP of the post-season Orlando Classic in 1988, which enabled him to be drafted by the Phoenix Suns with the seventh pick in the first round. After four years with the Suns, he was traded to the Philadelphia 76ers with Jeff Hornacek and Andrew Lang for Charles Barkley. Perry has spent three years with the Sixers. In 1996, he was traded to the New Jersey Nets along with Shawn Bradley and Greg Graham for Derrick Coleman, Sean Higgins and Rex Walters. During the summer months, Perry participates in the Charles Baker League.

Year	G	Pts.	Reb.
1984-85	30	2.3	3.9
1985-86	31	11.6	9.5
1986-87	36	12.9	8.6
1987-88	33	14.5	8.0
Career	130	10.5	7.6

Temple's Tim Perry was a great all-around low post player during his college career. Perry was a fine scorer, rebounder, and defensive player. In fact, he blocked 392 shots in his career.

DAVE WOHL

Dave Wohl teamed up with Steve Bilsky to form a famous Penn backcourt combination. Wohl, a 6-2, 185-pound guard, was a great jumpshooter. He scored a career total of 1,226 points. In 1970, he led the Quakers to a sensational 28-1 record and a No. 3 ranking in the country. He shot 83.7 percent from the free throw line during his career. Wohl's great foul shooting sealed a lot of victories for the Quakers.

Wohl spent seven years in the NBA with the Philadelphia 76ers, Portland Trail Blazers, Buffalo Braves, Houston Rockets and New Jersey Nets. After a few short stints as an NBA assistant coach, he became the head coach of the New Jersey Nets in 1985 for three years. He is currently the Executive Vice President of the Miami Heat's basketball operations. He is in his second tenure with the Heat, having served as a scout prior to the inaugural season, an assistant coach during Miami's first three years and the team's radio and television analyst in 1991-92.

Penn's Dave Wohl was the playmaker behind the 1970-71 team that went 28-0 and advanced to the Eastern Regional Final.

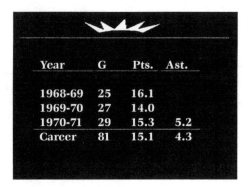

Year	G	Pts.	Ast.
1968-69	25	16.1	
1969-70	27	14.0	
1970-71	29	15.3	5.2
Career	81	15.1	4.3

JOE BRYANT

Joe Bryant, a two-time All-Big 5 player, was a multi-talent for La Salle. Bryant, a 6-10, 200-pound forward, could handle the ball, shoot from the perimeter, rebound and lead the fastbreak. A Philadelphia schoolboy legend at John Bartram High, he led the 1974-75 Explorers to the NCAA tournament with a 22-7 record.

In 1975, he left school a year early to pursue an NBA career. Bryant played eight seasons in the NBA with the Philadelphia 76ers, San Diego Clippers and the Houston Rockets. He also played professionally in Italy, Spain and France.

Upon his return to the United States, Bryant became involved in community affairs and also coached in the Sonny Hill League. He has conducted clinics in Philadelphia and the suburbs, and has served as the girls' coach at Akiba Hebrew Academy in Merion, PA and boys' junior varsity coach.

Until he resigned in May of 1996, Bryant served as an assistant coach at La Salle. His daughter Shaya plays volleyball for La Salle. Joe's wife Pam is the sister of former Villanova guard John

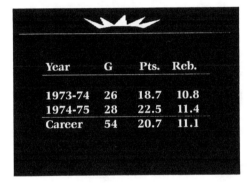

Year	G	Pts.	Reb.
1973-74	26	18.7	10.8
1974-75	28	22.5	11.4
Career	54	20.7	11.1

(Chubby) Cox. His son, Kobe, was named the No. 1 high school player in the country in 1996.

Bryant picked up the nickname "Jellybean" while playing for a champion John Bartram High team. Kids gave him bags of jellybeans while he watched first games of Palestra twinbills.Bryant is a member of the Big 5 Hall of Fame.

"I've played in the NBA and in Europe," Bryant said, "but it's nothing like playing in the Big 5. The games were always intense. And you never knew what could happen."

La Salle's Joe Bryant dazzled many Big 5 fans at the Palestra with his ballhandling and spectacular play around the basket.

AARON McKIE

A aron McKie finished his three-year stint at Temple tied for sixth on the school's all-time scoring list. Among those at Temple who played three years at Temple, only NBA great Guy Rodgers scored more points (1,767).

McKie, a 6-5, 209-pound guard, averaged 18.8 points a game while leading the Owls to the NCAA tournament his senior year. He was named to the Atlantic 10 Conference first team and was the only player to rank in the conference's top 10 in six statistical categories. In 1992-93, he received the Geasey Award as Big 5 MVP and was named the A-10 Player of the Year. He also averaged 20.5 points in four NCAA tournament games while carrying the Owls to the Elite Eight.

McKie teamed up with Eddie Jones to form the best one-two punch in college basketball. Both McKie and Jones were first-round draft picks of the Portland Trail Blazers and the Los Angeles Lakers respectively.

An obsessive worker, McKie made himself stronger and quicker each year. In early June, Aaron and Eddie got Temple players to help them prepare for 1995-96.

"I don't know anybody who works harder than Aaron," Jones said. "He always stayed after practice to work on his game. He played a lot of basketball during the offseason. Aaron has improved his game each year. Basically, he's done everything through practice and hard work."

Aaron McKie led Temple to three consecutive NCAA tournament appearances during his career. McKie was also named Big 5 MVP and Atlantic 10 Conference Player of the Year.

Year	G	Pts.	Reb.
1991-92	28	13.9	6.0
1992-93	33	20.6	5.9
1993-94	32	18.8	7.2
Career	92	17.9	6.4

NATE BLACKWELL

Nate Blackwell was the first big recruit of John Chaney's coaching career at Temple. Blackwell, a 6-4, 190-pound guard, put Temple basketball back on the map. The former Philadelphia Public League standout from South Philadelphia High School is fourth on the Owls' all-time scoring list with 1,708 points.

He led Temple to four consecutive NCAA tournament appearances from 1983 to 1987. He played in the backcourt with two outstanding players, Terence Stansbury and Howard Evans. He was named the Big 5's MVP in 1987. He received first-team All-Big 5 and Atlantic 10 Conference honors. In his senior year, Blackwell averaged 19.8 points a game and was named second-team All-America by *Basketball Weekly*.

"People asked me how I could play 40 minutes and never get tired," he once said. "I never got tired because I never really did any running."

In 1987, Blackwell was a second-round pick of the San Antonio Spurs. He spent some time with the Spurs and Golden State Warriors before starting his coaching career. Blackwell is currently an assistant basketball coach at Temple University.

Year	G	Pts.	Reb.
1983-84	31	7.2	1.8
1984-85	31	11.8	3.2
1985-86	31	13.1	3.9
1986-87	36	19.8	4.5
Career	129	13.2	3.4

Temple's Nate Blackwell received All-American honors his senior year with the Owls. In 1987, he led Temple to a brilliant 32-4 record.

THE BIG 5'S GREATEST COACHES

ig 5 coaches have been nothing short of magnificent. A number of NBA coaches started in the Big 5, including Jack Ramsay, Jimmy Lynam, and Chuck Daly. These successful coaches have tremendous basketball knowledge and also retain many strong local ties. Because a number of Big 5 coaches are from the Philadelphia area and have played for local schools, they know most of the high school coaches, players, summer leagues, and other key people in the Philadelphia basketball scene.

Big 5 coaches have done more with less than any other coaches in the country. The Big 5 coaches don't often sign the McDonald's or Parade All-American players. They usually take the top players in the Philadelphia area and develop them into solid college players. Here's a look at some of the top coaches in the Big 5, past and present.

DON CASEY

on Casey, an assistant coach with the New Jersey Nets, made his coaching mark as a Big 5 coach at Temple. Casey was the Owls' head man from 1973-74 through 1981-82, compiling a terrific 151-94 record during those seasons. Temple finished first or second in the East Coast Conference in his last seven years, and he posted 20 or more wins three times. His 1978-79 team, which finished 25-4, was the school's finest record since the 1957-58 season.

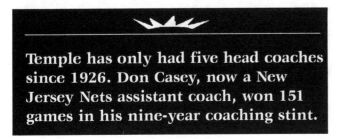

Temple has only had five head coaches since 1926. Don Casey, now a New Jersey Nets assistant coach, won 151 games in his nine-year coaching stint.

Casey was voted East Coast Conference Coach of the Year twice in his career. He guided the Owls to one NCAA postseason tournament and three NIT appearances. He took one of his Temple teams to Tokyo to play UCLA in the first NCAA game ever to be played out of the United States.

He coached an ECAC All-Star team on a tour of Yugoslavia after the 1978-79 season. Casey also developed a reputation as an expert in coaching against zone defenses and wrote a book entitled, *Temple of Zones.*

Casey learned a great deal about the college game from the legendary Harry Litwack, who coached the Owls for 21 years. He eventually succeeded Litwack in 1973. As Litwack's assistant for six years, Casey was a major contributor to the NIT championship team, which defeated Bob Cousy's Boston College Eagles in the 1969 championship game. Casey also helped Litwack secure NCAA berths in 1967, 1970, and 1972.

In 1982, Casey joined the NBA ranks as Paul Westhead's assistant with the Chicago Bulls, then held the same position with Jim Lynam's Los Angeles Clippers the following year. In 1984-85, Casey left the NBA to become a head coach in Italy, he returned to the Clippers as an assistant under Don Chaney and then Gene Shue for the next three seasons.

Casey replaced Shue as the Clippers' head coach in 1989 and held the post for a little more than a year. Under Casey's direction, the Clippers finished 30-52, but improved by nine wins from the previous season. The following year, the Clippers finished 41-85 under his leadership.

In 1990, Casey became an assistant coach with the Boston Celtics. He spent six years there before moving on to the New Jersey Nets.

JOHN CHANEY

John Chaney is one of the few head coaches to go from a predominantly black college to a major Division I institution. Chaney was an outstanding basketball coach at Cheyney State, where he spent 10 years coaching the Wolves. In 1978, he led Cheyney State to the NCAA Division II championship. Peter Liacouras, Temple University president, wanted someone to build the Owls' basketball program into a national powerhouse. Liacouras knew that man was John Chaney.

In 1982, Chaney took over an Owls' basketball program that hadn't won an NCAA tournament game since 1958. Chaney's first year at Temple was his most difficult season, due to several injuries. Nevertheless, he still

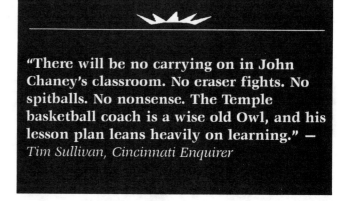

"There will be no carrying on in John Chaney's classroom. No eraser fights. No spitballs. No nonsense. The Temple basketball coach is a wise old Owl, and his lesson plan leans heavily on learning." — *Tim Sullivan, Cincinnati Enquirer*

Three-time national Coach of the Year John Chaney has led his Temple teams to 16 NCAA games and three times advanced to a regional final: in 1988, 1991, and 1993.

finished with a 14-15 record, including upsets over St. Joseph's and Rutgers in the first Atlantic 10 tournament at the Spectrum.

Only six schools have more victories than Temple's total of 1,435: North Carolina, Kentucky, Kansas, St. John's, Oregon State and Duke. Under Chaney, the Owls are a mainstay on the national scene, making several national television appearances, recruiting players nationwide and almost always receiving a bid to the NCAA tournament.

On the following page is the report card on Chaney over the years:

The *Seattle Post-Intelligencer* polled 13 Division I coaches to see who they felt "regularly does the best job under the most difficult circumstances," such as lack of facilities, resources, etc. The winner was John Chaney.

- Temple has played in 12 NCAA tournaments and in 14 straight postseason tournaments. The school had never participated in back-to-back NCAA tournaments, but in 1984, 1985, 1986, 1987 and 1988, and again in 1990, 1991, 1992, 1993, 1994, 1995 and 1996, the Owls participated in consecutive NCAAs.

- Temple has won 16 NCAA games and three times advanced to a regional final: in 1988, 1991 and 1993.

- Temple had a remarkable five-year stretch from 1983-88 when it won 25 or more games each year, winning 140 and losing just 23.

- Temple has won four Atlantic 10 regular season titles (in 1983-84, '86-87, '87-88 and '89-90) and four conference tournament championships (in 1985, '87, '88 and '90).

- Temple has won or shared nine Philadelphia Big 5 championships.

Chaney, 62, has three times been named national Coach of the Year. During the 1986-87 season, the United States Basketball Writers Association unanimously selected Chaney for the honor following Temple's 32-4 season.

The following year, Chaney was the consensus National Coach of the Year as the Associated Press, United Press International, CNN/USA Today, U.S.B.W.A., Kodak, and Chevrolet panels all selected Chaney as their top coach. That year he led the Owls to their best-ever 32-2 season and Temple was ranked No. 1 in the final polls. Chaney won another Coach of the Year award with Cheyney in 1978.

Chaney is the fourth-winningest active Division I men's basketball coach. His 23-year collegiate record stands at 540 wins and 188 defeats. He recently signed a five-year contract extension, good news for Temple basketball fans.

Three-time National Coach of the Year John Chaney has guided the Owls to an average of 23 wins per season and has taken 12 of his first 13 Temple teams into postseason competition.

"John Chaney's legendary sermons challenge the mind to question the status quo and to look for new solutions. His business card may read 'basketball coach,' but his area of expertise extends well into life off the court." —*Michael Bradley*

CHUCK DALY

Chuck Daly received a lot of publicity for coaching the 1992 U. S. Olympic Dream Team. He also obtained quite a bit of recognition for leading the Detroit Pistons to the 1989 and 1990 NBA championships. In addition to being voted into the Naismith Basketball Hall of Fame, Daly amassed a 564-379 record and a sensational 74-48 mark in the playoffs.

But Daly's best work may have been done on the collegiate level. In fact, Daly is regarded as the most successful coach in the 75 years of Pennsylvania basketball. He has the best winning percentage (.766 125-38), has won the most Big 5 titles (three), taken Penn to more NCAA tournaments (four), and ranks second only

Chuck Daly won 77 percent of his games at Penn before moving on to two NBA championships and the Olympics. He is one of 10 Big 5 coaches to become an NBA head coach.

Chuck Daly has won more Big 5 titles than any other coach.

to Lon Jourdet, in number of Ivy League titles won, six to four.

Penn was Ivy League and Big 5 titlist winning 53 of 56 games prior to Daly's appointment to follow Dick Harter. Under the pressure generated by his success, Daly won 25 of 28, directed the Quakers to the dual conference titles, won Eastern Coach of the Year honors, and Penn finished No. 1 in the East and third in the nation.

Daly won Ivy League championships in 1973, 1974 and 1975 following the initial title, and two Big 5 (1973, 1974) titles were added. Over the next two years, Penn won 17 of 26 games and was an Ivy League and Big 5 contender despite a rash of injuries. The following season, Daly had a young team, but was still able to compete for the Ivy League title. He finished his Penn career with an 18-8 record, then became a key assistant to new 76ers coach Billy Cunningham.

FRAN DUNPHY

Now in his eighth season with the Quakers, Dunphy is one of the most respected coaches in college basketball. His Penn record is 123-65. In 1994-95, he guided the Quakers (22-6) to their third consecutive undefeated Ivy League season.

Dunphy took over the Penn program in April 1989 after serving as an assistant to Tom Schneider. After posting records of 12-14 and 9-17 in his first two seasons as head coach, Dunphy's hard work and quality recruiting paid off in 1991-92. The Quakers went 16-10, including a stretch of 14 wins in the last 18 games.

Following a 22-5 Ivy championship season in 1992-93, Dunphy took his 1993-94 team one step further. That season, Penn posted a 25-3 record and not only advanced to the NCAA tournament, but eliminated Nebraska in the first round. In addition, Dunphy led the Quakers to their first appearance in the Associated Press Top 25 since 1979. In the 1994-95 season, Penn repeated as Ivy League champions and lost to Alabama in the first round of the NCAA tournament. In 1995-96, Penn finished with a 17-10 record, but did not advance to the NCAA tournament.

Penn head coach Fran Dunphy has compiled a 123-65 record in his seven years coaching the Quakers.

Fran Dunphy led Penn to an unprecedented third consecutive undefeated Ivy League season in 1994-95; Penn was the first team since UCLA in the 1970s to do so. Penn won 48 consecutive games until Dartmouth ended the streak with a 54-53 win over the Quakers on February 9, 1996.

DICK HARTER

Big 5 connections have helped the coaching career of former Penn coach Dick Harter, who is currently serving as an assistant with the Portland Trail Blazers. Harter, 63, made his NBA debut as an assistant coach under another former Penn coach, Chuck Daly, in 1983-84. Following a three-year stint in Detroit, Harter served for two seasons (1986-87 and 1987-88) as an assistant under Dr. Jack Ramsay with the Indiana Pacers.

In 1988 Harter was named the first head coach of the Charlotte Hornets. He guided the Hornets during the franchise's first year and a half. Harter also assisted Pat Riley with the New York Knicks from 1991 to 1994.

Prior to his NBA tenure, Harter enjoyed an 18-year collegiate coaching career, compiling a 295-193 record with Rider College (1965-66); Penn, his alma mater (1966-67 through 1970-71); Oregon (1971-72 through 1977-78) and Penn State (1978-79 through 1982-83).

Harter's teams went 53-3 during his final two seasons at Penn. He earned Eastern Basketball Coach of the Year honors in 1971, when Penn ranked third in the nation with a 28-1 mark. Overall, Harter compiled a combined head coaching record of 319-287.

Dick Harter is one of three former Penn head coaches who were also NBA head coaches. Harter was head coach of the Charlotte Hornets from 1988-90.

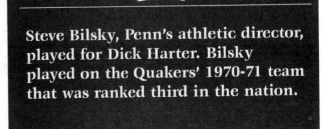

Steve Bilsky, Penn's athletic director, played for Dick Harter. Bilsky played on the Quakers' 1970-71 team that was ranked third in the nation.

JACK KRAFT

Jack Kraft spent 12 years as the head coach of the Villanova Wildcats, with an impressive 238-95 record. He's guided six teams to the NCAA tournament and five to the NIT.

In 1971, he took his team all the way to the NCAA finals in Houston. The Wildcats defeated St. Joseph's, Fordham, Penn and Western Kentucky before losing to perennial champion UCLA. Kraft was elected Coach of the Year by his peers. In 1972, Kraft's team made it to the NCAA Eastern Regionals for the third straight year.

Kraft was Eastern Coach of the Year three times. Final rankings have placed his teams in the top 10 on several occasions, and he has coached such professional basketball stars as Wali Jones, Jim Washington, Bill Melchionni, Chris Ford, Howard Porter, and Tom Ingelsby. He won the Quaker City Tournament twice, the Big Five three times and the Holiday Festival.

In 1973, he left Villanova to become head coach at the University of Rhode Island, where he had a 123-96 record. Kraft is retired and living in Stone Harbor, N.J.

Jack Kraft was voted Eastern Coach of the Year three times.

Jack Kraft was inducted into the Big 5 Hall of Fame in 1987.

STEVE LAPPAS

Steve Lappas' overall coaching record of 135-108 indicates that he's done a great job of rebuilding the Wildcats' basketball program. In just four seasons, he has put Villanova basketball back into the national spotlight. A year ago, the Wildcats advanced to the NCAA tournament posting a 26-7 record.

In 1994-95 the Wildcats won their first-ever Big East Conference Tournament championship and tied a school record with 25 victories. Villanova returned to the NCAA for the first time since 1991 and finished the season with a No. 9 Associated Press ranking.

Lappas was presented in 1995 with the Harry Litwack Award as Eastern Coach of the Year by the Philadelphia Sportswriters Association, earned Big 5 Coach of the Year, and was a finalist for AP and Naismith College Coach of the Year.

Lappas also guided Villanova to its first ever National Invitation Tournament championship in 1994. In only his second season with the Wildcats, they won 14 of their final 17 games, finishing with a 20-12 record. For his achievements during the

"Winning the (1985) championship was an incredible experience. I don't think I appreciated it right away, since it was my first season. But as I look back on it now, it's one of the biggest experiences of my life." —
Steve Lappas

1994 season, Lappas was voted Coach of the Year in the East Region by *Basketball Times* and received a Special Recognition Award from the Philadelphia Big 5.

He was named Villanova's seventh head men's basketball coach in 1992. Lappas came to Villanova from Manhattan College where he earned Metro Atlantic Athletic Conference Coach of the Year in 1992 after guiding the Jaspers to a 25-9 overall record, their best finish in school history, and a third-round NIT appearance.

Prior to his successful seven-year run as a head coach, Lappas made his debut as an assistant for Rollie Massimino in 1984-85. Throughout his four years as an assistant, Lappas helped guide the Wildcats to the national championship in 1985.

HARRY LITWACK

Harry Litwack provided a lot of national exposure for Temple's basketball program. "The Chief" led the Owls to 13 postseason tournaments in 18 years before retiring in 1993, after his Owls posted a 17-10 record for their 14th consecutive winning season. Litwack's 1969-70 team also captured the MAC title to make the NCAA Tournament.

Litwack led the Owls to an overall 22-8 record and the National Invitation Tournament championship in 1969. Some of his brightest moments came in the late '50s and early '60s. Litwack's teams produced four All-Americans: Hal Lear won first-team honors in 1956 and Guy Rodgers earned the same accolades in 1957 and 1958. Bill (Pickles) Kennedy was Temple's All-American in 1960-61, and John Baum, captain of the 1969 NIT champions, was also cited.

Rodgers and Kennedy, along with former Temple assistant coach Jay Norman, starred on Litwack's 1957-58 team, which is considered by many the best Temple has ever put on the court. That team had a 27-3 record and rolled up 25 straight wins for the longest streak in the nation that season. Litwack guided the Owls to third-place finishes in the 1956 and 1958 NCAA Tournaments and the 1957 NIT.

Litwack became an institution at Temple and is a member of the school's Hall of Fame. He finished his career with a 373-193 record over 21 years, and was inducted into the Naismith Basketball Hall of Fame in 1975. Litwack has also been inducted into the Pennsylvania, South Philadelphia High School and Big 5 Halls of Fame.

Harry Litwack coached Guy Rodgers and Hal Lear considered by many experts as one of the best backcourts in college basketball history.

Harry "The Chief" Litwack's remarkable run as a Temple player, assistant coach and head coach spanned six decades. It included 373 victories, two Final Fours, an NIT championship and an induction into the Naismith Hall of Fame.

JIM LYNAM

Jim Lynam was hired by John Nash, former Washington Bullets general manager, to be the team's head coach in 1994. Nash, former Executive Director of the Big 5, had always been impressed with Lynam's coaching expertise.

"I had the opportunity in my career to work with some of the best coaches in the history of the game including Chuck Daly, Jack Ramsay, Paul Westhead, Billy Cunningham and Rollie Massimino to name a few," Nash said. "Jim Lynam embodies qualities found in all five. . ."

Lynam left coaching after the 1991-92 season to become the general manager of the 76ers. He had coached the previous four-and-a-half seasons, becoming the second-winningest coach behind Billy Cunningham, compiling a 194-173 record.

Lynam coached the 1989-90 Sixers team to a 53-29 record and the Atlantic Division title. The division title was the first for Philadelphia since winning the NBA championship in 1983. He had been with the Sixers organization since 1985, when he was hired as an assistant to head coach Matt Guokas. He joined the Sixers with four years of professional coaching experience.

Lynam began his NBA coaching career in Portland during the 1981-82 season as an assistant to his former college coach Jack Ramsay. He became head coach of the San Diego/Los Angeles Clippers during the 1983-84 season and compiled a 30-52 record. In his second year, he was re-

Jim Lynam learned a great deal about the game from his former college coach Jack Ramsay. Lynam was hired as head coach by the Washington Bullets in 1994.

placed 61 games into the season with a 22-39 record.

His college coaching career covered 10 seasons (with a 158-118 record). His career included two seasons at Fairfield University (23-29), five seasons at American University (70-61), and three at St. Joseph's (65-28).

Lynam's .699 winning percentage at St. Joseph's is the second best in school history, behind only Ramsay. During his stint with the Hawks, they made two NIT appearances and were Mideast runner-up in the 1981 NCAA Tournament following a major upset over No. 1 ranked DePaul. Lynam is a member of the St. Joseph's and Big 5 Hall of Fame.

ROLLIE MASSIMINO

Rollie Massimino, former Villanova coach, will enter his first season as coach of Cleveland State this year. Massimino, who left Villanova in 1992, spent two years coaching at the University of Nevada, Las Vegas. He spent two seasons coaching the Running Rebels to a 21-6 and 15-14 record, respectively, before working as a television commentator for college basketball games. Massimino spent 19 years (1973-1992) at Villanova, compiling a 357-241 record.

Massimino amassed a total of 16 postseason appearances, including 12 NCAA tournament bids and five appearances in the Final Eight. The national championship in 1985 was a major accomplishment.

Massimino reached the pinnacle of his coaching career when the Wildcats shot an NCAA Tournament record 78.6 percent (22-28 FGs) from the field, and shocked Georgetown, 65-64, for the 1985 title. Massimino spent the last two years doing some color commentary on Atlantic 10 Conference basketball.

Former Villanova coach Rollie Massimino is entering his first season as head coach of Cleveland State.

Rollie Massimino's biggest accomplishment was leading the 1985 Villanova Wildcats to the national championship.

JACK McCLOSKEY

Jack McCloskey, who two years ago retired as general manager of the Minnesota Timberwolves, excelled as a player and coach at the University of Pennsylvania. A native of Mahoney City, Pennsylvania, McCloskey graduated from Penn in 1948. During his playing days with the Quakers, he participated in basketball, football, and baseball. After that, he played eight years in the American and Eastern Basketball League. His career also includes a brief stint in the NBA and four years of professional baseball in the Philadelphia Athletics organization.

McCloskey became head coach of the Quakers' basketball program in 1956, inheriting a 7-19 team. He turned the team around, posting 13-12 and 12-14 records and then putting together seven consecutive winning seasons with Ivy League first-place finishes annually.

In his last season, McCloskey led the 1965-66 Penn team to a 19-6 slate, the most wins since 1954-55, and captured the Ivy League championship. His teams were 87-53 in Ivy League competition and won the Big 5 title in 1963. He finished with a 146-105 record in 10 Penn seasons.

McCloskey's next move was to rebuild a lowly Wake Forest team into an Atlantic Coast Conference contender. After a 14-39 record in his first two seasons as the Demon Deacons head coach, he followed with four successful seasons in the rugged ACC. With assistants Billy Packer and the late Neil Johnston, scoring champion for the old Philadelphia Warriors, McCloskey compiled a 56-50 record before moving to the NBA.

McCloskey spent some time as a coach with the Portland Trail Blazers, Los Angeles Lakers and the Indiana Pacers. However, he's best known for playing a key role in constructing the Detroit Pistons' NBA championships in 1989 and 1990.

Jack McCloskey is one of 18 Quakers to be inducted into the Big 5 Hall of Fame.

Jack McCloskey is one of the few Big 5 coaches who has worked as a coach and general manager in the NBA.

JACK McKINNEY

Jack McKinney, like so many St. Joseph's basketball coaches, learned the game from Dr. Jack Ramsay. McKinney had the opportunity to play for Ramsay at Hawk Hill.

After his playing career was finished, it all began for McKinney in 1958 at St. James High School in Chester where he coached track and field and basketball. He led St. James to a basketball runner-up position in 1960 in the Philadelphia Catholic League.

In 1960, McKinney returned to St. Joseph's as assistant athletic director and freshman basketball coach. In five years as mentor, he compiled a record of 59-18 and two Big 5 titles. His 15-1 mark in the 1963-64 campaign with Cliff Anderson stands as the best freshman record ever at St. Joseph's.

In 1965, McKinney became head coach at Philadelphia Textile. In his only season there, he led the Rams to a 21-

Jack McKinney is one of six St. Joseph's players to go on to head coaching careers in the NBA.

Jack McKinney, former St. Joseph's coach has excelled on all coaching levels: high school, college and professional.

6 slate and a berth in the NCAA College Division Tournament.

When Ramsay joined the Philadelphia 76ers as general manager in 1966, McKinney returned to St. Joseph's as athletic director and basketball coach. With Cliff Anderson the only starter returning from Ramsay's glory teams of 1964-65 and 1965-66, McKinney fashioned a small hustling team in the Hawk tradition and finished with a 16-10 record.

He led St. Joseph's to an impressive five NCAA Tournament appearances. He also was named Coach of the Year in his conference in both 1973 and 1974.

McKinney helped Jack Ramsay guide Portland to the 1977 NBA title. He was Magic Johnson's first NBA coach, but was seriously injured in a bicycle accident and Paul Westhead took the Lakers to the 1980 crown. In 1981, he was named NBA Coach of the Year with the Indiana Pacers.

BILL "SPEEDY" MORRIS

ill "Speedy" Morris was a Philadelphia coaching legend before he arrived at La Salle. In 14 seasons at Philadelphia's Roman Catholic High School, he achieved a 347-82 record. He won one Philadelphia City championship; six Philadelphia Catholic League championships; two National Catholic Tournament championships, and had four 30-win seasons. Morris then spent two years as head coach of Philadelphia's William Penn Charter where he posted a 41-14 record. His 1984 team won the Philadelphia Interacademic League championship.

Morris came to La Salle for the 1984-85 season when he replaced Kevin Gallagher as head coach of the Explorers' women's program. His women's teams won 22 games in 84-85 and 21 games in 85-86. The 1985-86 team won the Metro Atlantic Athletic Conference title and advanced to the NCAA tournament.

Following that season, Morris replaced Dave (Lefty) Ervin as the men's basketball coach, becoming the first Division I coach to make such a major change. Morris led his first Explorer team to a 20-13 record and into the championship game of the postseason NIT. His 1987-88 team compiled a 24-10 record, went 14-0 in the Metro Atlantic Athletic Conference and swept through the MAAC Tournament to earn the conference's NCAA Tournament berth.

In 1988-89, Morris took the Explorers to another level with a 26-6 record, including a regular season league championship and the conference tournament crown again. In 1989-90, Morris guided the Explorers to a 30-2 record, the most victories by any La Salle team in history and a school record of 22 consecutive wins, their third straight MAAC regular season championship, the MAAC tournament crown and a third consecutive NCAA berth.

The NCAA tournament victory over Southern Mississippi in Hartford in 1990 was Morris' 100th as La Salle's men's coach. Only three other Division I coaches have won that many games in their first four seasons: current Syracuse coach Jim Boeheim; North Carolina State's legendary coach of the late '40s and early '50s, Everett Case; and most recently, Roy Williams of Kansas.

In 1990-91, the Explorers battled through injuries and the graduation loss of National Player of the Year Lionel Simmons to a 19-10 record and a berth in the NIT, where La Salle lost a 93-90 heartbreaker at Massachusetts.

The 1991-92 season saw Morris guide La Salle to its sixth consecutive postseason appearance and its fourth conference title and NCAA tournament berth in five years. In 1993, when La Salle upset Big 5 rival St. Joseph's, 66-53, Morris earned his 146th La Salle men's coaching victory and surpassed Ken Loeffler on the Explorers' all-time victory list. Morris' career coaching record to date stands at 614-232, including men's college basketball (177-95 with La Salle's men's team), women's college basketball (43-17 as La Salle's women's coach) and boys' high school (347-82 at Roman Catholic and Penn Charter).

His winning percentage in his ten years as La Salle's men's coach puts him 35th on the winningest active Division I coaches list (by percentage and with a minimum of five years at a Division I school).

DR. JACK RAMSAY

When you talk about great coaches in the Big 5, Dr. Jack Ramsay's name immediately comes to mind. Ramsay, currently a color commentator on the NBA for ESPN, started his head coaching career at St. Joseph's in 1955.

In his first season, Ramsay led the Hawks to a 23-6 record, the school's first Big 5 championship, and a trip to the National Invitation Tournament, the school's first postseason tourney. St. Joseph's had a powerhouse team that season with All-Big 5 performers Mike Fallon, Bill Lynch, Al Juliana and Kurt Engelbert. Ramsay stayed at St. Joseph's for 11 years, compiling a record of 234-72 with seven appearances in the NCAA tournament and three in the NIT. Ramsay also guided the Hawks to six Big 5 championships.

In 1966, the intense Ramsay left coaching because of a stress-induced eye problem. He was hired by Irv Kosloff to be the general manager of the Philadelphia 76ers. In his first season there, the 76ers won an NBA-record 68 games enroute to the world championship. After a year in the front office, Ramsay returned to the sidelines. The 76ers went 55-27 in 1969, and Ramsay led them to the playoffs three out of four years.

Dr. Jack Ramsay compiled a 234-72 record in his eleven years at St. Joseph's helm.

Jack Ramsay led St. Joseph's to six Big 5 championships.

He moved to the Buffalo Braves as head coach in 1972, and in four years there took teams into the playoffs three times.

Ramsay became the head coach of the Portland Trail Blazers in 1976-77. He inherited a team that not only had never made the playoffs, but had never produced a winning record. In his first year there, he guided the Trail Blazers to a 49-33 mark and the NBA championship. He followed that season with a 58-24 mark in 1977-78, the best record in the league. In 10 seasons at Portland, his teams made the playoffs nine times.

Ramsay was named the Indiana Pacers' head coach in 1986. In two years, the Pacers compiled a 79-74 record, including one appearance in the NBA playoffs. After an 0-7 start in 1988-89 season, Ramsay decided to step down.

In 21 NBA seasons he won 864 games (trailing only Lenny Wilkens and Red Auerbach). He was on the sideline for 1,649 games as an NBA coach, a league record. Add 300 victories in 17 years on the college and high school levels, and Ramsay has won an incredible 1,164 games.

AL SEVERANCE

The late Al Severance was the head coach of the Villanova Wildcats for 25 years. Between 1936 and 1961, he compiled a 416-202 record with trips to the NCAA Tournament in 1939, 1949, 1951 and 1955. Severance's 1939 team advanced to the Final Four, and the 1959 and 1960 Wildcats went to the NIT. Moreover, Severance coached as a founding member of the Big 5 (1955-61). He was also a faculty member at Villanova and a Justice of the Peace during his coaching career with the Wildcats.

Former Villanova coach Al Severance huddles with his players. Severance is the most successful coach in Villanova basketball history.

Al Severance was inducted into the Big 5 Hall of Fame in 1994.

BOB WEINHAUER

Bob Weinhauer, former vice-president of basketball operations for the Houston Rockets, now an assistant coach with the Milwaukee Bucks, had a very successful run as head coach of the University of Pennsylvania. In his five years as the Quakers' head coach, he had three 20-plus winning seasons. Of course, the highlight of his career was guiding Penn to the 1979 NCAA Final Four, the last such appearance by an Ivy League team. His Quakers made four trips to the NCAA tournament and one to the NIT.

In 1983, he left Penn to become head coach at Arizona State. In three years with the Sun Devils, he posted a 41-45 record. Following that, Weinhauer had a short stint in the CBA as the head coach of the Detroit Spirits. Since then, he has served in a player personnel and scouting capacity with several NBA teams such as the Philadelphia 76ers, the Washington Bullets, the LA Clippers and the Minnesota Timberwolves.

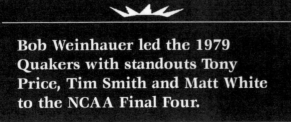

Bob Weinhauer led the 1979 Quakers with standouts Tony Price, Tim Smith and Matt White to the NCAA Final Four.

PAUL WESTHEAD

Paul Westhead, currently the head coach of George Mason's basketball team has the distinction of not only playing, but also coaching in the Big 5. Westhead played on three NCAA tournament teams at St. Joseph's under Jack Ramsay.

His first coaching job was as an assistant at the University of Dayton in 1963. The next year, he was named basketball coach at Cheltenham High School on the outskirts of Philadelphia. He spent four years at Cheltenham before returning to St. Joseph's as an assistant athletic director and freshman basketball coach.

Westhead started his career as a head coach in 1970 at La Salle. In his first season, the Explorers put together a 20-7 mark and were invited to the NIT. During his nine-year career at La Salle, Westhead's teams won 142 games and twice played in the NCAA tournament (1975 and 1978).He left La Salle in 1979 to become an assistant coach for the Los Angeles Lakers under Jack McKinney. Westhead became the Lakers' head coach after McKinney was injured in a bicycle accident and was unable to coach.

He took over and led the Lakers to the NBA championship that defeated Julius Erving and the

Philadelphia 76ers in a six-game series. In the sixth game, Magic Johnson, playing center in place of the injured Kareem Abdul Jabbar, took the Lakers to the championship.

L.A. was 50-18 under Westhead during the regular season and 12-4 in the playoffs. The following year, he coached the Lakers to a 54-28 record and the Pacific Division title. After 11 games into the next season, he was replaced by Pat Riley.

He went on to become the head coach of the Chicago Bulls for the 1982-83 season. In 1985, Westhead took over as the head coach of the sport's highest scoring games in history.

Loyola Marymount went to the NIT in Westhead's first season. He also carried Loyola Marymount to NCAA appearances, including advancing to the Final Eight in 1990. He coached former Philadelphia Public League stars Bo Kimble and the late Hank Gathers at Loyola

Marymount, who were a big part of those high scoring games. In fact, Kimble and Gathers came home to play against two Big 5 foes, La Salle and St. Joseph's during the 1989-90 season.

Westhead left Loyola Marymount in 1990 to coach the Denver Nuggets for two seasons. After spending two years with the Nuggets, he took a year off to conduct some clinics in Italy, Spain, Greece and Australia.

Westhead, a Shakespearean scholar, decided to get back into coaching college basketball. In 1993, he became the head coach of George Mason's basketball team. He is presently trying to build the Patriots into a winning program after posting three disappointing seasons. Westhead's overall college record is 264-190. His NBA coaching record is 159-164.

BIG 5 PLAYERS IN ACTION

Penn's Paul Little (right), Karl Racine (left) and George Noon (second left) smother Villanova's Ed Pinckney (center) during a Big 5 game at the Palestra. Noon was a solid role player for the Quakers. Racine and Little both received All-Big 5 honors during their careers. Racine was one of the best ballhandlers in the Ivy League. Little was a tough all-around player, who could play defense, shoot, rebound and take the ball to the basket. Pinckney was MVP of the Big 5 in 1985. He led Villanova to a Big 5 and NCAA championship that year. *Photo by Ed Mahan.*

Penn's Chris Elzey (20) goes in for a score in an Ivy League matchup against Yale. Elzey was not a flashy player. He relied on fundamentals and great jumpshooting to help the Quakers. In fact, Elzey's outside shooting helped Penn win some games in the Ivy League. Elzey played for two different coaches during his career: Craig Littlepage and Tom Schneider. *Photo by Ed Mahan.*

Temple's Alton McCullough (33) moves into position for a rebound against St. John's at the Palestra. McCullough scored a career total of 1,051 points. He was a great inside player. McCullough could rebound, score and play good defense. He played for then head basketball coach Don Casey at Temple. He played on one NCAA tournament team and two NIT teams. McCullough played with some great players like Ricky Reed, Bruce Harrold and Keith Parham. *Photo by Ed Mahan.*

Alton McCullough led the Temple Owls to the NCAA tournament in 1982.

Penn's Chris Elzey (20) grabs a rebound over St. Joseph's James Owens in a Big 5 game at the Spectrum. Owens was one of the Big 5's great leapers. He was known for his spectacular dunks. Elzey didn't possess the foot speed and leaping ability of most players. Nevertheless, he knew how to position himself for rebounds. Elzey wasn't afraid to go inside and compete against bigger players. He grabbed a lot of rebounds in close games for the Quakers. These rebounds ended up leading Penn to victory. *Photo by Ed Mahan.*

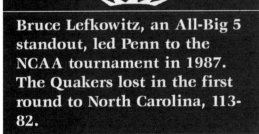

Bruce Lefkowitz, an All-Big 5 standout, led Penn to the NCAA tournament in 1987. The Quakers lost in the first round to North Carolina, 113-82.

Penn's Bruce Lefkowitz (24) goes up for two points. Lefkowitz was an All-Big 5 and All-Ivy League standout with the Quakers. He was known for his scrappy play around the basket. He led Penn in rebounding each of his four years. Lefkowitz also led the Quakers in field goal accuracy throughout his career. He scored a career total 1,443 points. Lefkowitz grabbed a game-high 23. *Photo by Ed Mahan.*

Penn's Abe Okorodudu (center), Villanova's Harold Pressley (21) and Dwight Wilbur (4) maneuver for rebounding position under the basket. Pressley and Wilbur were members of the Wildcats' 1985 NCAA championship team. In 1986, Pressley was named first team All-Big 5. He was named the Big 5's Most Valuable Player that year. Pressley led Villanova to the second round of the NCAA tournament his senior year. He was also a first-round pick of the Sacramento Kings in 1986. He is currently playing professional basketball in Spain. *Photo by Ed Mahan.*

Tim Claxton was named first-team All-Big 5 along with Michael Brooks (La Salle), Keith Herron (Villanova), Keven McDonald (Penn) and Marty Stahurski (Temple) in 1978.

Temple's Tim Claxton glides to the basket during a Big 5 game against Villanova at the Palestra. Claxton was an All-Big 5 standout with the Owls. He scored 1,418 points in his collegiate career. Claxton played for Temple coach Don Casey, who is now an assistant coach with the New Jersey Nets. In 1977-78, he led the Owls to a 24-5 record and a bid to the NIT. He also helped Temple win the Big 5 championship. Claxton is one of the many Philadelphia Public League stars to play for Temple. *Photo by Dennis Savage.*

Temple's Walt Montford (44) takes a jumpshot against Penn in a Big 5 game at the Palestra. Montford is one of the Owls' all-time leading scorers. He finished his career with 1,067 points. He averaged 11.0 points a game his senior year. Montford played with Temple standouts Rick Reed, Keith Parham and Alton McCullough. In 1978-79, he led Temple to a 25-4 record and a spot in the NCAA tournament. He also enabled the Owls to share a part of the Big 5 championship with Penn. *Photo by Ed Mahan*

Walt Montford is #17 on Temple's all-time game scoring list. He scored 35 points in 1977 against Buffalo with 13 field goals and nine free throws.

Temple's Keith Parham shoots from long range during a game at the Palestra. Parham is the son of Philadelphia basketball great Tee Parham. He scored 1,092 points in his career with the Owls. His senior year, he averaged 13.4 points a game. In 1980-81, he teamed with Neal Robinson to lead the Owls to a 20-8 record and a bid to the NIT. Temple also shared the Big 5 championship with St. Joseph's, Penn, La Salle and Villanova. *Photo by Ed Mahan.*

Temple's Keith Parham, Alton McCullough (33) and Mark Davis (31) play defense against St. Joseph's during a Big 5 game at the Civic Center. Parham, McCullough and Davis played for Temple Coach Don Casey, who was the Owls' head man from 1973-1982. McCullough was known for his solid inside play, scoring and defense. Parham was one of the Owls' best outside shooters. Davis was a fine defensive and open court player. *Photo by Ed Mahan.*

In 1985, St. Joseph's Bob Lojewski was drafted in the 5th round of the NBA draft by the Sacramento Kings.

St. Joseph's Bob Lojewski (44) looks for an opening against Villanova's Harold Jensen (22) in a Big 5 game at the Palestra. Jensen played a huge role in the Wildcats' run for the NCAA championship in 1985. He made a lot of big shots in Villanova's big win over Georgetown for the national title. Lojewski received second-team All-Big 5 honors in 1985. His outside shooting carried the Hawks to a 19-12 record and a spot in the NIT. *Photo by Ed Mahan.*

La Salle's Albert (Truck) Butts goes up for two points in the lane against St. Peter's in a Metro Atlantic Athletic Conference game at the Palestra. Butts played with Steve Black and Ralph Lewis, two former Public League standouts at La Salle. He received second-team All-Big 5 honors in 1984. Butts carried the Explorers to a 20-11 record and a piece of the Big 5 title in 1984 with Temple. He was known for his rebounding, scoring and defense. *Photo by Ed Mahan.*

La Salle's Albert Butts scored 1,060 total points for a 12.0 average in 88 games from 1981-84.

La Salle's Chip Greenberg (20) takes a jumpshot against Villanova. Greenberg received All-Big 5 honors in 1986. He played with some great players such as Steve Black, Ralph Lewis, Tim Legler and Albert Butts. Greenberg scored 1,227 points in his years at La Salle. He played in the NCAA tournament in 1983. He also participated in the NIT in 1984. *Photo by Ed Mahan.*

Temple's Granger Hall (30) intercepts a pass for Villanova's Harold Pressley (21). Also shown is Temple's Terence Stansbury (43) during a Big 5 game at the Palestra. Hall, Pressley and Stansbury are currently playing professional basketball in Europe. Hall led Temple to a 25-6 record and a bid to the NCAA tournament. He was voted first-team All-Big 5 in 1985. Hall had reconstructive knee surgery early in his college career, but he was able to come back and have a fine career. *Photo by Ed Mahan.*

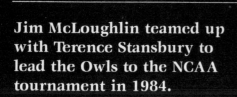

Jim McLoughlin teamed up with Terence Stansbury to lead the Owls to the NCAA tournament in 1984.

La Salle's Larry Koretz (44) and Ralph Lewis (11) battle for a rebound under the basket. Lewis was named MVP of the Big 5 in 1984. Koretz was known for his outside shooting. He played on the Explorer team that advanced to the NIT finals in 1987. Lewis was a versatile player. He had the ability to play guard as well as forward. Lewis finished his career with 1,807 points. Koretz scored 1,382 points in his career. *Photo by Ed Mahan.*

La Salle's Steve Black shoots from long range during a Big 5 game against Penn at the Palestra. Black scored a Big 5-record 40 points against Temple in a 1983 game. He tallied 2,012 points in his career. Black is one of three 2,000 point scorers in La Salle's basketball history. The other two players are Tom Gola and Michael Brooks. Black received All-Big 5 honors three consecutive years. He is also a member of the Big 5 Hall of Fame. *Photo by Ed Mahan.*

Alex Bradley is on Villanova's all-time highest free throw percentage list, shooting 12-12 vs. Penn State on February 4, 1979.

Villanova's Alex Bradley (42) takes a short jumper from the corner. Bradley scored 1,634 points in his collegiate career. He received All-Big 5 honors in 1979 and 80. Bradley led Villanova to a 23-8 record and a spot in the NCAA tournament in 1980. He is a member of the Big 5 Hall of Fame. After graduating from Villanova, Bradley played one season for the New York Knicks. *Photo by Ed Mahan.*

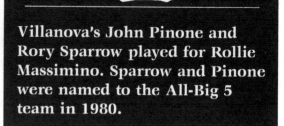

Villanova's John Pinone and Rory Sparrow played for Rollie Massimino. Sparrow and Pinone were named to the All-Big 5 team in 1980.

Villanova's John Pinone (45) goes for a rebound during a Big East game at the Palestra. Pinone was voted MVP of the Big 5 three consecutive years. He led Villanova to a 24-8 record and a Big 5 championship in 1983. Pinone also carried the Wildcats to the NCAA tournament his senior year. He scored 2,024 points in his career. Pinone played one year for the Atlanta Hawks in 1983-84. *Photo by Dave Coskey.*

St. Joseph's Jeffery Clark (12) shoots a jumper around Villanova's Alex Bradley (42). Clark shared MVP honors of the Big 5 with Villanova's John Pinone in 1982. Clark led St. Joseph's to two consecutive NCAA tournament apearances in 1981 and 1982. He played in the backcourt with Bryan Warrick. Clark played for head coaches Jim Lynam and Jim Boyle during his collegiate career. Bradley is one of Villanova's all-time leading scorers and rebounders. He finished his career with 797 rebounds. *Photo by Ed Mahan.*

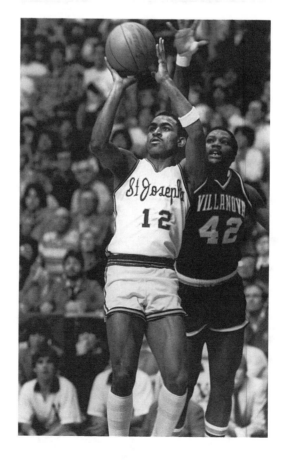

Villanova's Alex Bradley (42) gets position underneath the basket for a rebound. Bradley played in the same frontcourt with John Pinone. Both players received All-Big 5 honors in their careers. Bradley played for former Villanova head coach Rollie Massimino. *Photo by Ed Mahan.*

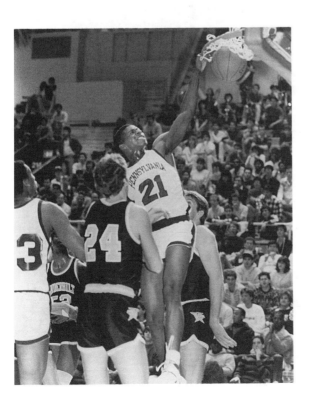

Tyrone Pitts is in Penn's 1,000 point club with 1,301 career points from 1984-88, and a 12.3 point per game average.

Penn's Tyrone Pitts slam dunks two points during a non-conference game against Vanderbilt at the Palestra. Pitts was known for brilliant open court play with the Quakers. He averaged 17.4 points and 7.0 rebounds in 1988. He scored 1,301 points in his career. He played for head coaches Craig Littlepage and Tom Schneider. Pitts made one trip to the NCAA tournament during his career.
Photo by Ed Mahan.

Temple's Tim Perry (33) out jumps La Salle's Lionel Simmons (22) during a Big 5 game at the Palestra. Simmons plays for the Sacramento Kings. Simmons scored 3,217 points in his college career. He was named Player of the Year in 1990. Perry played on Temple's 1987-88 No. 1 ranked team. He was named Player of the Year in the Atlantic 10 Conference. *Photo by Ed Mahan.*

Tim Perry and Granger Hall played on Temple's 1984 Big 5 championship team.

Villanova's Reggie Robinson moves into defensive position. Robinson was one of the Wildcats' top defensive players. He scored 1,309 points and grabbed 559 rebounds in his career. Robinson played four years under former Villanova head coach Rollie Massimino. In 1978, he led the Wildcats to a 23-9 record and a spot in the NCAA tournament. Robinson was one of the Wildcats' most versatile players. He could shoot from the perimeter, handle the ball and play solid defense from the forward position. *Photo by Ed Mahan.*

Gary McLain, along with Ed Pinckney and Dwayne McClain formed the "Expansion Crew," which led Villanova to its first national title on April 1, 1985.

Villanova's Gary McLain (22) looks for an open man. McLain received All-Big 5 honors in 1985. He played a key role in Villanova's drive to the national championship. McLain was the starting point guard on the NCAA championship team that included Ed Pinckney, Dwayne McClain, Dwight Wilbur and Harold Pressley. McLain dished out 546 assists in his career. He made the All-NCAA championship team his senior year. *Photo by Ed Mahan.*

Penn's John Wilson (10) guards former Villanova guard Veltra Dawson during a Big 5 game at the Palestra. Dawson played two years with the Wildcats before transferring to Evansville. Wilson provided the Quakers with a steady ballhandler in the backcourt. He played for the 1986 Pennsylvania team that advanced to the NCAA tournament.

Wilson played for head coaches Craig Littlepage and Tom Schneider. He played with former Quaker standouts Perry Bromwell, Tyrone Pitts, and Bruce Lefkowitz during his career. *Photo by Ed Mahan.*

St. Joseph's Maurice Martin (11) drives on Temple's Nate Blackwell (3) during an Atlantic 10 Conference game at the Palestra. In 1985 Martin led St. Joseph's to the A-10 and Big 5 championships. Martin was a first-round pick of the Denver Nuggets. He was voted into the Big 5 Hall of Fame in 1992. In his senior year, he carried the Hawks to the NCAA tournament with a 26-6 record under former head coach Jim Boyle. Martin scored 1,726 points in his career. *Photo by Ed Mahan.*

Temple's Granger Hall (30) and Villanova's Ed Pinckney (54) are prepared to move into rebounding position. Pinckney and Hall had some great battles in City Series games at the Palestra. Both players received All-Big 5 honors in 1985. In addition, Pinckney and Hall are both members of the Big 5 Hall of Fame. Hall led the Owls to the NCAA tournament in 1985. Pinckney guided Villanova to the national championship in 1985. *Photo by Ed Mahan.*

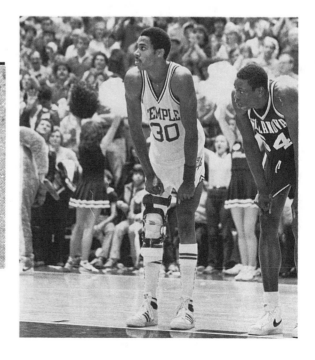

St. Joseph's Jeffery Clark (12) guards Temple's Kevin Broadnax (22) during a Big 5 game at the Palestra. Clark had the ability to find the open man. He played excellent defense; he usually played the other team's best scorer in the backcourt. Clark is St. Joseph's all-time steals leader with 250. He also has the highest free throw percentage of any St. Joseph's player with .837. Clark is currently a basketball official in the Philadelphia Public League.
Photo by Ed Mahan.

In 1988, Mark Plansky led Villanova to the NCAA's Final Eight. The Wildcats defeated Arkansas, Illinois and Kentucky in the tournament before losing to Oklahoma (78-59).

Villanova's Mark Plansky plays defense during a Big 5 game at the Spectrum. Plansky was a member of the Wildcats 1985 NCAA championship team. He was known for his brilliant outside shooting, defense and rebounding. Plansky scored 1,217 points in his career. In his senior year, he led Villanova to a 24-13 record and a trip to the NCAA tournament. In 1988, he received second-team All-Big 5 honors.
Photo by Ed Mahan.

Temple's Ramon Rivas (44) shoots a baseline jumpshot during a Big 5 game against Penn. Rivas played on Temple's No. 1 ranked team in 1988 which included Tim Perry, Mike Vreeswyk, Mark Macon, Howard Evans and Duane Causwell. Rivas was known for his inside play and monstrous picks to free Temple shooters. He is currently playing professional basketball in Spain. Rivas played one season with the Boston Celtics.

Ramon Rivas led the Temple Owls to a 4-0 record and the Big 5 City Series championship in 1988.

Temple's Charles Rayne (34) slams home two points against La Salle. Rayne was voted to the All-Big 5's second team in 1985. He was known for his spectacular dunks. Rayne was a fine defensive player for the Owls. He played with some terrific players such as Nate Blackwell, Terence Stansbury, Granger Hall, Tim Perry and Howard Evans. Rayne led Temple to back-to-back NCAA appearances in 1984 and 85. *Photo by Ed Mahan.*

St. Joseph's James (Bruiser) Flint (14) dribbles against Duke's Tommy Amaker during a non-conference game at the Palestra. Flint received All-Atlantic 10 Conference honors in 1987. He dished out 402 assists in his career. Bruiser Flint is the head coach at the University of Massachusetts; Amaker is an assistant coach at Duke. Flint was a member of the 1985 St. Joseph's team that won the Big 5 and Atlantic 10 championships.
Photo by Ed Mahan.

Bruiser Flint is fifth on St. Joseph's all-time career assists list with 402.

Villanova's John Pinone (45) moves toward the basket during a Big East game against Syracuse. Pinone had the ability to get outstanding position around the basket. He did a good job of using his size to score and get some key rebounds for the Wildcats. Pinone was one of the top players in the Big 5 and the Big East throughout his career. *Photo by Ed Mahan.*

John Pinone is tied with Alex Bradley for highest free throw percentage, going 12-12 vs. St. Joseph's on February 28, 1981.

Villanova's Rory Sparrow (3) drives to the basket against St. Bonventure. Sparrow received All-Big 5 honors in 1980. He also played nine years in the NBA with New Jersey, Atlanta, New York, Chicago and Miami. Sparrow scored 1,183 points in his career. He was one of the best clutch shooters in Villanova basketball history.

St. Joseph's Bernard Blunt (12) celebrates with the fans following a huge Big 5 victory over Temple at the Hawks' Alumni Fieldhouse. Also shown (left) former St. Joseph's head coach John Griffin.Blunt is the Hawks' all-time leading scorer with 1,985 points. In his senior year, he led the Hawks to a 17-12 record and trip to the NIT. Blunt's scoring talents also helped St. Joseph's earn a share of the Big 5 title with Temple in 1995. *Photo by Ed Mahan.*

Villanova's Keith Herron (33) goes up for two points during a non-conference game against the University of Massachusetts. Herron led Villanova in scoring three consecutive years. Herron led Villanova to a 23-9 record and a spot in the NCAA tournament. He received first-team All-Big 5 honors with Michael Brooks (La Salle), Tim Claxton (Temple), Keven McDonald (Penn) and Marty Stahurski (Temple). He played four years (1978-82) for the Atlanta Hawks, Cleveland Cavaliers and the Detroit Pistons. *Photo by Ed Mahan.*

Villanova's Keith Herron (33) shoots over two Notre Dame defenders. Herron scored 2,170 points during his career with the Wildcats. He is the school's all-time leading scorer. Herron was named to the NCAA All-East Region team. He played four years under former Villanova head coach Rollie Massimino. *Photo by Ed Mahan.*

Villanova's Keith Herron received All-Big 5 honors in 1976, '77, and '78.

Villanova's Harold Pressley (21) shoots a jumpshot from the corner during a game at the Palestra. Pressley was named MVP of the Big 5 in 1986. He is Villanova's all-time career steals leader with 213. In 1986, he carried the Wildcats to a 23-14 mark and a trip to the NCAA tournament. He was a first draft pick of the Sacramento Kings. He played four years (1986-90) for the Kings. Pressley averaged 16.8 points and 10.2 rebounds his senior year. *Photo by Ed Mahan.*

Villanova's Ed Pinckney (54) slam dunks two points during a game at the Palestra. Also shown are Villanova's Dwayne McClain (33, lower left) and Harold Pressley (behind Pinckney). Pinckney, Pressley and McClain were all starters on Villanova's 1985 national championship team. Pinckney recently finished his 11th season in the NBA. McClain played one season with the Indiana Pacers. He is currently playing professional basketball in Australia. Pressley spent four years with the Sacramento Kings. He is now playing professional basketball in Spain. *Photo by David Zeft.*

La Salle's Albert (Truck) Butts looks to make a move against Penn in a Big 5 game at the Palestra. Butts' fine inside play helped the Explorers tie Temple for the Big 5 City Series championship in 1984. He received All-Big 5 honors in his career. In 1984, he led the Explorers to a 20-11 record and an appearance in the NIT. Butts played on the same team with Big 5 standouts Ralph Lewis and Steve Black. *Photo by Ed Mahan.*

La Salle's Larry Koretz (44) shoots a long jumper from the corner. Koretz's brilliant outside shooting led the Explorers to the NIT Finals in 1987. Koretz scored 1,382 points in his career. *Photo by Ed Mahan.*

La Salle defeated Villanova, 86-84 in the first round of the NIT in 1987.

La Salle's Steve Black glides in for a slam dunk against Notre Dame at the Palestra. Black received All-Big 5 honors in 1985. He scored a career total 2,012 points. Black is the fourth all-time leading scorer at La Salle behind Tom Gola, Michael Brooks and Lionel Simmons. He set a Big 5 record by scoring 40 points in a 84-79 loss to Temple. In 1985, he averaged 19.7 points a game. As a freshman, he led all first-year players with a 20-point scoring average. *Photo by Ed Mahan.*

La Salle's Ralph Lewis (11) shoots over two defenders during a game at the Palestra. Lewis made the Explorers basketball team as a walk-on from Philadelphia's Frankford High School. He is one of the top basketball players in Explorer history. In 1991, he was inducted into the Big 5 Hall of Fame. Lewis scored 1,807 in points his career. As a junior, he received Big 5 MVP honors averaging 20.6 points and 9.1 rebounds a game. *Photo by Ed Mahan.*

La Salle's Ralph Lewis played on the Detroit Pistons' 1987-88 team coached by former Penn mentor Chuck Daly.

St. Joseph's Geoff Arnold (12) handles the ball against Villanova's Dwight Wilbur during a Big 5 game at the Palestra. Arnold's ball-handling skills led the Hawks to the Atlantic 10 Conference championship and to the NCAA tournament in 1986. Arnold was one of the top playmakers in the Atlantic 10 and the Big 5. He played with two former St. Joseph's stars Maurice Martin and Rodney Blake, who helped to lift the Hawks into the NCAA tournament. Arnold is currently an assistant basketball coach at the University of Massachusetts under head coach James "Bruiser" Flint. *Photo by Ed Mahan.*

Temple's Ed Coe (4) drives past a George Washington defender in Atlantic 10 action. Coe received All-Big 5 honors in 1986. He scored 1,177 points in his career. He averaged 15.6 points his senior year. Coe's all-around talents led Temple to a 25-6 record and a spot in the NCAA tournament. He played with former Temple stars Granger Hall, Nate Blackwell, Howard Evans and Tim Perry. In 1985, Coe scored a career-high 26 points to help Temple record a 81-73 Big 5 victory over Villanova.

Temple's Jim McLoughlin (15) and Granger Hall (30) move into the Owls' vaunted zone defense. McLoughlin and Hall led the Owls to the NCAA tournament in 1984. McLoughlin played in the backcourt with Terence Stansbury, the second leading scorer in Temple basketball history. McLoughlin scored a career total of 1,124 points. He averaged 11.4 points a game his senior year. Hall was an outstanding forward for the Owls. He received All-Atlantic 10 Conference and honorable mention All-America honors his senior year.
Photo by Ed Mahan.

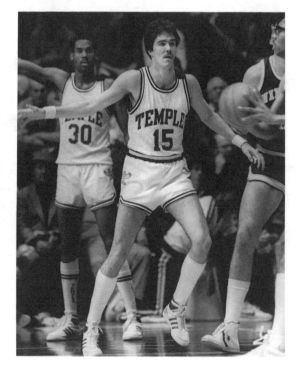

Temple's Jim McLoughlin (15) looks for the open man. Also pictured is Temple's Alton McCullough (33). McLoughlin and McCullough played their high school basketball in Delaware Dary Township High School. McLoughlin was a star at Collingdale High School. Both players scored over 1,000 points in their college careers. McLoughlin played for head coaches Don Casey and John Chaney. McCullough played his entire career under Casey. *Photo by Ed Mahan.*

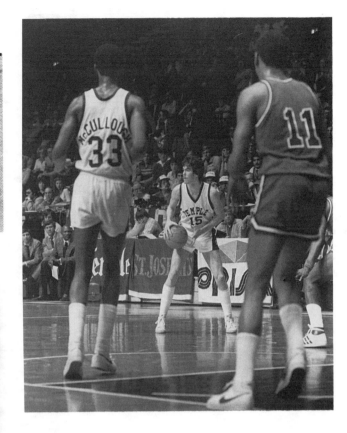

Jim McLoughlin holds the Temple record for three-point shot attempts in one game. In the 1982-83 season, he made 18 three-point attempts against Rutgers.

Temple's Ricky Reed (21) lays in two points. Reed shared MVP honors with Penn's Tony Price in 1979. Reed scored 1,031 points in his career. He averaged 15.7 points a game his senior year. In 1979, he led Temple to a 25-4 record and a trip to the NCAA tournament. Reed was also noted for his ballhandling and passing talents. He dished out 546 assists in his career. He's second on the all-time assists list behind Howard Evans. *Photo by Ed Mahan.*

Temple's Ed Coe looks to make a pass during a game at the Palestra. Coe's outside shooting and hustling defense carried Temple to the NCAA tournament his senior year. In 1986, he grabbed some key rebounds and made some big shots to help Temple post a 61-50 overtime win over Jacksonville in the NCAA tournament. *Photo by Ed Mahan.*

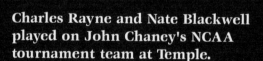

Charles Rayne and Nate Blackwell played on John Chaney's NCAA tournament team at Temple.

Temple's Charles Rayne (34) shoots over a West Virginia defender during an Atlantic 10 Conference game at the Palestra. Also pictured is Temple's Nate Blackwell (3). Rayne scored 1,131 points in his career. Rayne and Blackwell led the 1984 to the NCAA tournament. Blackwell scored 1,708 points in his career. He received All-Atlantic 10 Conference and All-America honors. He was drafted by the San Antonio Spurs on the second round in 1987. *Photo by Ed Mahan.*

Granger Hall was a dominant player and a big man on campus. He returned from a serious knee injury to be an honorable mention All-American and an Atlantic 10 Conference Player of the Year.

Temple's Tim Perry (33) waits for the foul shot to be taken. Perry was named Atlantic 10 Conference Player of the Year in 1988. In his senior year, he led the Owls to the No. 1 spot in the college basketball polls. Perry, Mark Macon, Howard Evans, Ramon Rivas and Mike Vreeswyk guided Temple to the NCAA Final Eight in 1988. Perry blocked 392 shots in his career. *Photo by Dave Zeft.*

Temple's Granger Hall (30) and La Salle's Ralph Lewis (11) move into rebounding position during a Big 5 game at the Palestra. Hall, an All-Big 5 performer, is currently playing professional basketball in Europe. Lewis, a terrific player for La Salle, played on the 1988 Detroit Pistons team that went to the NBA finals. Temple and La Salle had some great battles at the Palestra. *Photo by Ed Mahan.*

St. Joseph's Tony Costner (23) grabs a rebound in a Big 5 game against Villanova at the Palestra. Costner, a 6-10 center, was inducted into the Big 5 Hall of Fame in 1990. Costner is currently playing professional basketball in Europe. In 1984, Costner scored 25 points as St. Joseph's defeated Penn, 86-66 at the Palestra. He tied the Hawk single-game scoring mark when he tallied 47 against Alaska-Anchorage on December 30, 1983 in the consolation game of the Cable Car Classic. *Photo by Ed Mahan.*

Tony Costner, former St. Joseph's standout, played his scholastic basketball at Philadelphia's Overbrook High School.

St. Joseph's Steve Donches (14) was the Hawks' super-sub who hit a 29-foot jumpshot to beat Villanova, 71-69 at the Palestra. The Hawks' brilliant reserve hit one of the biggest shots in Big 5 history. Donches played with St. Joseph's stars Matt Guokas and Cliff Anderson. His coach was Jack Ramsay. In 1966, St. Joseph's was crowned as the City Series champion largely because of Donches' great shot.

St. Joseph's Tony Costner (23) takes a shot from the free throw line during Big 5 action. Costner scored 1,729 points and grabbed 951 rebounds in his career. In 1984, Costner's scoring and rebounding helped St. Joseph's post a 20-9 record and land a spot in the NIT. Costner shot over 50 percent from the field throughout his career. He played his scholastic basketball at Philadelphia's Overbrook High School. *Photo by Ed Mahan.*

Norman Black was inducted into the St. Joseph's Hall of Fame in 1984.

St. Joseph's Norman Black (24) grabs a rebound during a game at the Palestra. Black received All-Big 5 honors in 1977. In 1985, he was inducted into the Big 5 Hall of Fame. Black and Maurice Martin finished with their careers as the fifth all-time leading scorers. Both players have scored 1,726 points. Black snared a career total 906 rebounds. *Photo by Ed Mahan.*

St. Joseph's Marcellus "Boo" Williams slam dunks two points for the Hawks against Lafayette. Williams received All-Big 5 honors in 1980. He was inducted into the Big 5 Hall of Fame in 1987. Williams finished as one of St. Joseph's top 10 all-time leading scorers with 1,554 points. In 1980, he led St. Joseph's to a 21-9 record and a trip to the NIT. *Photo by Dennis Savage.*

Boo Williams, ex-St. Joseph's star currently runs a summer basketball program in his hometown of Hampton, Virginia.

Marcellus "Boo" Williams celebrates after St. Joseph's wins the Big 5 City Championship over Villanova in 1980. Williams scored 27 points and shot 11-for-11 from the free throw line in a 60-56 Big 5 victory over Penn at the Palestra. He played a huge role in the Hawks' drive for the City Series title. In 1980, Williams enabled St. Joseph's to capture its first Big 5 championship since 1968. *Photo by Ed Mahan.*

Boo Williams has coached NBA standouts Alonzo Mourning and Dennis Scott and 76ers rookie Allen Iverson in his summer basketball league.

Villanova's Ed Pinckney (54) moves into position for a rebound against St. Joseph's Bryan Warrick. Also pictured is Villanova's Dwayne McClain. St. Joseph's and Villanova have played in some exciting Big 5 games over the years. St. Joseph's-Villanova rivalry has been one of the biggest in Big 5 history. Pinckney, McClain and Warrick had some great Big 5 battles at the Palestra. *Photo by Ed Mahan.*

Villanova's Stewart Granger handles the ball with defensive pressure from St. Joseph's Jeffery Clark. Granger was a first-round draft pick of the Cleveland Cavaliers. He is also a member of the Big 5 Hall of Fame. Granger scored 1,307 points in his career. He dished out a career total of 595 assists for the Wildcats. In 1981, he led Villanova to a 20-11 record and a spot in the NCAA tournament. *Photo by Ed Mahan.*

Stewart Granger was named first-team All-Big 5 in 1981.

Temple's Terence Stansbury showcases his ball-handling skills. Stansbury and backcourt mate Jim McLoughlin guided the jumper to send Temple into its first overtime with La Salle in 1984. The Explorers eventually won the game 80-79 in double overtime at the Palestra. Stansbury also hit a 22-foot jumper at the buzzer to lead Temple over St. John's in the NCAA tournament. He was one of great clutch shooters in Temple basketball history. *Photo by Ed Mahan.*

Penn's Perry Bromwell (4) drives to the basket against Villanova's Harold Jensen (32). Bromwell received All-Big 5 and All-Ivy League honors during his career. He scored 1,265 points in his career. He has the highest three-point field goal percentage in school history. During his three-year varsity career, he shot 50.6 from three-point range. In 1987, Bromwell's fine all-around play led Penn to the NCAA tournament. *Photo by Ed Mahan.*

St. Joseph's Wayne Williams looks for an open man. Williams was a key player on the Hawks' 1986 Atlantic 10 and Big 5 championship team. He received second-team All-Big 5 honors in 1986 and 87. Williams scored 1,048 points in his career. He also shot 47.7 percent from the field throughout his playing days at St. Joseph's.

Perry Bromwell led Penn to the Ivy League championship in 1987.

Maurice Martin was a first-round pick of the Denver Nuggets in 1986.

St. Joseph's Maurice Martin (11) passes the ball to Bob Lojewski (44) during a game at the Palestra. Lojewski scored 1,682 points and grabbed 724 rebounds in his career. Martin ranks second among St. Joseph's all-time top five in points, assists, steals, blocked shots and field goal percentage. Both players received All-Big 5 honors during their careers. *Photo by Ed Mahan.*

THE BIG 5'S GREATEST VICTORIES

In 1985, Villanova shocked the college basketball world by defeating Georgetown and capturing the NCAA championship. The Wildcats played the perfect game and became the toast of college basketball. Craig Miller, former Villanova sports information director, was there at Rupp Arena when Rollie Massimino led the Wildcats to the national title. Portions of this chapter were taken from his game story.

This game was one of the biggest upsets in college basketball. Villanova, which had lost twice during the regular season to Georgetown, pulled off the school's greatest victory. Rollie Massimino's Wildcats shocked defending champion Georgetown, 66-64.

It was Ed Pinckney, Dwayne McClain and Gary McLain, "The Expansion Crew." And it was a solid team effort with Harold Pressley, Harold Jensen and Dwight Wilbur being most noticeable. "Everyone wrote us off, didn't think we had a chance to win," Massimino said. "Every one of you (media) people said we had no shot, shouldn't even play the game. No one thought we could do it, but I did and so did they.

"After we had our Mass this morning, I did something I've never done before. I sent the kids back upstairs and asked each one to spend 15 minutes totally by himself, thinking about the game and two

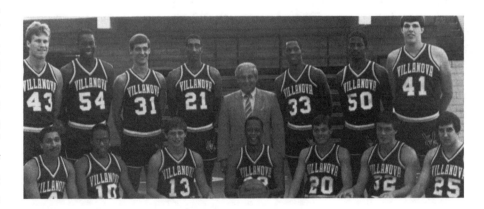

The 1984-85 Villanova Wildcats (l to r): Dwight Wilbur, Veltra Dawson, R.C. Massimino, Gary McLain, Brian Harrington, Harold Jensen, Steve Pinon. Standing: Wyatt Maker, Ed Pinckney, Mark Plansky, Harol Pressley, Head Coach Rollie Massimino, Dwayne McClain, Connally Brown, Chuck Everson.

things. One was play to win, don't play to lose. And the other was, Hey, we're good enough to win. On a one-shot deal, we can beat anyone in the United States."

And on that day (April 1, 1985) Villanova was the best team in college basketball.

The Wildcats played great defense and controlled the tempo. Villanova sank an amazing 22 of 28 field goal tries for a sizzling 78.6 percent. Even more startling, in the second half the Wildcats connected on nine of 10 field goals; 90 percent field goal shots. From the foul line, the Wildcats went 22 of 27, including 11 of 14 in the last two minutes.

What made Villanova's shooting performance

It was April 1, 1985, when David met and beat Goliath. It was a game remembered by many as one of the most perfectly played NCAA championship games ever. It was a game few felt the undermanned Villanova Wildcats had much of a chance of winning.

even more impressive was whom it was accomplished against. Patrick Ewing, David Wingate, Reggie Williams and the Georgetown Hoyas were the No. 1 defensive team in the country and had limited opponents to just 39 percent shooting from the field for the entire season.

"It was frustrating," Georgetown guard Horace Broadnax said. "We kept playing defense. We were right in their faces and they kept hitting and hitting."

Georgetown took some early leads on Villanova, but every time Villanova regrouped and rallied. Harold Pressley followed up his own missed shot with :04 left before the half, and Villanova went into the locker room, leading 29-28, while a CBS-TV audience stared in disbelief.

The Hoyas took the lead at 42-41. The lead changed hands five times until Villanova slipped out to a 53-48 advantage. But Georgetown roared back, and with 4:50 to go had a 54-53 lead and possession. Georgetown tried to spread the floor and run the clock.

However, Dwayne McClain, a player remembered for knocking down big shots in crucial moments came up with a big steal. Villanova patiently worked for a good shot. Freshman Harold Jensen nailed a 16-footer to give Villanova a 55-54 lead with 2:36 to play.

"I was totally open and I just shot in rhythm," Jensen would later explain. "They were so conscious of protecting against Ed inside that I had the shot."

Pinckney blocked David Wingate's driving baseline layup and was fouled retrieving the ball, and after both free throws, the Wildcats had a 57-54 lead. Villanova's ability to sink free throws produced a 65-60 lead with 18 seconds left. A Villanova free throw and two Georgetown layups made it 66-64 with two seconds left. Dwayne McClain, who had tripped and fallen, caught the inbounds pass on the floor and when the final two seconds ticked off the clock, the Wildcats were champions.

O n March 30, 1994, Villanova became the 15th Division I school to win both an NCAA and NIT championship, when the Wildcats defeated Vanderbilt 80-63 to grab the NIT title. The Wildcats' championship run capped a season that surpassed all expectations.

The Wildcats were led by Jonathan Haynes, who scored 19 points, and Kerry Kittles, who posted 18. Eric Eberz added 16 points and a team-high seven rebounds in the Wildcat victory. Both Haynes and Kittles were named to the All-Tournament team.

In the first half, Villanova had trouble getting untracked. Vanderbilt led by as many as 17 points, shooting 52 percent from the field and 60 percent from three-point range. Vanderbilt held a 15-point lead at halftime.

Center Jason Lawson celebrates the Wildcats' 1994 National Invitation Tournament Championship. The Wildcats recorded a 20-12 overall record en route to the NIT title in head coach Steve Lappas' second season at the helm of the Villanova program.

The second half was a completely different story. The Wildcats came out with determination, and outscored the Commodores 30-16 over the next 12 minutes to take a one-point lead with 8:22 remaining. Kittles led the scoring parade with 11 points, while Eberz contributed eight during the stretch.

At that point, it was a nip and tuck battle, with the Wildcats fighting back each time. With 4:19 left in the game and Vanderbilt holding a precarious 70-67 lead, Kittles hit a three-pointer to tie the game, and Vanderbilt would manage only one more basket in the game. Alvin Williams then took center stage, stealing a Billy McCaffrey pass that Haynes promptly converted into a three-pointer. Williams was there on the next Commodore possession as well with another steal and one foul shot.

The score then stood at 74-70, and the Wildcats were not to be denied. In the final 33 seconds of the game, Ron Wilson and Eberz each converted a pair of free throws and Williams scored on a layup as the clock wound down. Villanova had won an NIT championship in Madison Square Garden.

On March 22, 1969, Temple head coach Harry Litwack and team captain John Baum led the Owls to an NIT championship. Temple competed in the Middle Atlantic Conference during those years, and the conference championship was the ticket to the NCAA tournament.

The senior-laden 1968-69 team just missed receiving a bid to the NCAA tournament, losing to St. Joseph's on a buzzer-beating shot in overtime of the MAC championship game. The NIT came calling for the seventh time in the Litwack Era, and the Owls took advantage of their extended season.

Litwack, better known as "The Chief," had a starting lineup featuring Baum, an All-Big 5 and MAC standout, Eddie Mast, Joe Cromer, Bill Strunk and Tony Brocchi. The Owls defeated Florida in the NIT opener and followed that with a 94-78 win over St. Peter's. Then came a stunning victory over Tennessee, 63-58, in the semifinals.

Litwack made a key substitution late in the second half of the championship game against Boston College. With the Owls trailing 67-64, he called on Tom Wieczerak to spell Strunk, who was hobbling on a bad ankle, and the move ignited a 25-9 rally that produced an 89-76 victory and an NIT championship.

"This is the happiest day of my coaching life," Litwack said after the game.

THE BIG 5's GREATEST BACKCOURT

GUY RODGERS AND HAL LEAR

The Big 5 has produced a lot of great backcourt tandems over the years, such as Penn's Jerome Allen and Matt Maloney, Steve Bilsky and Dave Wohl; Temple's Nate Blackwell and Howie Evans, Villanova's Tom Ingelsby and Ed Hastings, and St. Joseph's Jeffery Clark and Bryan Warrick to name a few. However, the finest backcourt combination to ever play in this city is Temple's Guy Rodgers and Hal Lear.

Four years ago, Rodgers and Lear were honored at halftime of the matchup between Temple and Penn as a part of the Big 5's 40th anniversary team. They were also inducted into the Philadelphia Basketball Hall of Fame. Herm Rogul, former *Philadelphia Bulletin* sports columnist, profiled these great players in a Philadelphia Basketball Hall of Fame program. Portions of this story were taken from his interview.

Former Temple standouts Guy Rodgers (first left), Hal Lear (second left) and Jay Norman (first right) and Temple radio broadcaster Sonny Hill meet during a Big 5 Hall of Fame luncheon. *Photo by Ed Mahan.*

Temple's 1955-56 left-handed backcourt duo of sophomore Guy Rodgers and senior Hal Lear is still regarded as one of the greatest of all time in college basketball.

There have always been some great combinations in life such as peanut butter and jelly, milk and honey and bread and butter. But when it comes to Philadelphia basketball, there has never been a better backcourt combination than Guy Rodgers and Hal Lear.

They played only one college season together, leading Temple to a 27-4 record in 1955-56, capped by a 90-81 victory over Southern Methodist for third place in the NCAA Tournament. Lear set a Final Four record of 48 points in his finale.

"I first set eyes on Harold," Rodgers said, "when Northeast played Overbrook. He was great, but, of course, Northeast won. Even in high school, the sonofagun had the sweetest shot this side of heaven.

"We were both left-handed, but that was never a problem. We could each go down either side. Our friendship was the most special thing about playing with Hal."

Lear averaged 24.0 points as a senior, Rodgers 18.5 as a sophomore in 1955-56.

Rodgers became one of the NBA's greatest playmakers, collecting 10,415 points and 6,917 assists. In the NBA Register, his statistics appear between those of Oscar Robertson and Bill Russell.

Lear outscored such teammates as Bill Sharman, George Yardley and Bill Spivey with the Los Angeles Jets in the American Basketball League in 1961.

Mostly Lear put up big numbers in the Eastern League weekend wars in small cities. In 1964, the Philadelphia Bulletin's George Kiseda watched Lear shoot 19-for-24 for 42 points in the Camden Bullets' 126-118 win over the Wilkes-Barre Barons and asked why Hal wasn't in the NBA.

Rodgers and Lear led the Owls to the 1956 Final Four, with Lear scoring a still-standing school record 745 points (24. avg.) during the season, including 48 in the Final Four third-place game against SMU.

"They want to pay you something like $7,000 or less," Lear said. "I can make more than that working. Unless you get paid $15,000, it's not worth it."

By the time St. Louis and New York came after him, Lear had established himself in City Hall, preparing civil service examinations. Charles Baker, his uncle was Commissioner of Records. He suggested Lear get valuable work experience and save his jumpshot for weekends, not to mention Philadelphia summers.

Lear is an administrator at Albert Einstein Medical Center in New York City.

"We played together every summer in the Baker League," Rodgers said. "Hal was incredible! Back then, there was a quota on blacks in the NBA. Harold, John Chaney, Sonny Lloyd, Sonny Hill and many other Philadelphians could have played in the NBA."

Racism helped make Rodgers an Owl. Temple was one of the few major colleges that offered scholarships to black athletes.

"Some schools offered me scholarships," Rodgers said, "without knowing I was black. My mother wrote letters to ask if they accepted blacks and the answer was 'No.'

"A month before I was going away to college—I hadn't made up mind which one—my mother passed away. My mother had really wanted me to go to Temple because it was close to home."

Due largely to the dynamic duo of Lear and Rodgers, the Owls headed into their second-ever NCAA Tournament with a record of 23-3.

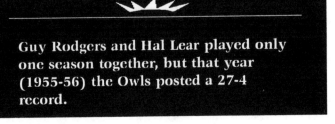

Guy Rodgers and Hal Lear played only one season together, but that year (1955-56) the Owls posted a 27-4 record.

Rodgers averaged 20.4 points with Mel Brodsky as his backcourt mate as the Owls went 20-9 in 1956-57 (third in the NIT) and averaged 20.1 with Bill "Pickles" Kennedy as his partner as Temple went 27-3 in 1957-58 (third in NCAA tourney). But his sophomore season remains special.

"We had Fred Cohen, Tink Van Patton, Danny Fleming, Hotsy Reinfeld, Jay Norman, Barry Goldstein, Leon Smith, Mel Brodsky, Billy Smith and John Gronozio," Rodgers said, from memory. Eddie Baron was our assistant coach.

"The fastbreak worked because we had guys hitting the boards and firing the outlet passes. Then Harold and I could fly. Jay and Hotsy and Tink never got the credit they deserved. Day in and day out, they worked hard and played tough defense. We didn't have a selfish man on that team.

"I was like the young kid on the team. When I was down, they picked me up. We looked up to the older guys. They were really helpful and I'm not just talking about basketball.

"We had one of the greatest coaches, ever, Harry Litwack. We had a group of players creating a masterpiece, like an oil painting with all of the colors coming together in the best way."

Rodgers, who resides in Los Angeles, is an avid Temple

Guy Rodgers averaged 18.5 points per game in his first collegiate season.

loyalist. He has led Owl support groups at Las Vegas and UCLA. He has also been impressed with the coaching of current Temple leader John Chaney.

"John Chaney is a great teacher," Rodgers said, "and he cares so much for his players, they respond to him."

Rodgers stays in contact with his good friend Sonny Hill, former CBS basketball commentator, who runs the Charles Baker League, the Hank Gathers College League, the Wilt Chamberlain High School League and the Bill Cosby Future League in Philadelphia.

"Sonny and I have been friends forever," Rodgers said. "I was the only one who could get him out of his house. His grandmother let him come out with me. He carried my bag because he wanted to. We shared milkshakes and hamburgers and fishcakes.

"Sonny is a loving and caring person. I'm 3,000 miles away, but we still communicate. We're long distance brothers. It was at the Fun Field that I told Sonny he had a chance to become an outstanding basketball player."

Hill still tells how proud he was that Guy Rodgers allowed him to carry Guy's bag.

For more than 40 years, the Big 5 has been known for producing outstanding guards. Hal Lear played for the Philadlephia Warriors from 1956-57. Guy Rodgers, the fifth pick in the first round of the 1958 NBA draft, ranks eighth on the all-time NBA assist charts with 6,917.

OTHER GREAT BIG 5 BACKCOURT COMBINATIONS

Matt Guokas and Billy Oakes
(St. Joseph's 1964-65)

Wali Jones and Billy Melchionni
(Villanova 1963-64)

Bruce Drysdale and Bill "Pickles" Kennedy
(Temple 1959-60)

Roland Taylor, Bernie Williams and Larry Cannon (La Salle 1968-69)

Steve Bilsky and Dave Wohl
(Pennsylvania 1970-71)

Matt Maloney and Jerome Allen
(Pennsylvania 1994-95)

Tom Ingelsby and Ed Hastings
(Villanova 1970-71)

Jeffery Clark and Bryan Warrick
(St. Joseph's 1980-82)

Nate Blackwell and Howard Evans
(Temple 1985-87)

Howard Evans and Mark Macon
(Temple 1987-88)

Doug Overton and Randy Woods
(La Salle 1990-91)

THE BIG 5's
GREATEST SCHOLAR-ATHLETE

N o one has demonstrated the qualities of being a student athlete better than former Pennsylvania captain John Edgar Wideman. Wideman led the Quakers to their first Big 5 title in 1963 and was named All-Big 5 and All-Ivy League.

His basketball skills were good enough for him to be named to the Big 5 Hall of Fame in 1974. But Wideman's greatest accomplishments did not come on the hardwood.

A Benjamin Franklin scholar, Wideman graduated Phi Beta Kappa in 1963. He became a Rhodes Scholar, the second African-American recipient ever.

He came back to Penn as an English professor in 1967 and stayed until 1972, when he left to pursue a career in writing. He is currently recognized more as an author than he was as a basketball player.

His 1984 book, *Sent For You Yesterday*, won the prestigious Faulkner Award and he was selected to deliver Penn's baccalaureate address in 1986.

John Wideman, voted All-Big 5 in 1963, received two Faulkner Awards for Fiction in 1984 and 1991.

He didn't stop there. In May of 1991, he received his second PEN/Faulkner Award for Fiction, this time for his book, *Philadelphia Fire*, about the burning of the MOVE headquarters in West Philadelphia.

Although Wideman thrilled many with his physical ability, he has reached so many more with his powerful gifts of the mind. The Big 5 has produced some fine student-athletes over the years who have received national recognition for their outstanding academic talents.

There are seven Academic All-Americans and four NCAA Graduate Scholars from the Big 5. The seven student-athletes are Penn's Bob Morse, Villanova's Tom Ingelsby, John Pinone and Harold Jensen, and La Salle's Tony DiLeo, Tim Legler and Jack Hurd. The four post-graduate scholars are St. Joseph's Charles McKenna, Morse, Hurd and Pinone.

Morse, a 1972 Penn graduate, played for Dick Harter and Chuck Daly during his college career. He played on the 1971 Quaker team, which posted a 28-1 record. In 1977, Morse, an All-Ivy League standout, was inducted into the Big 5 Hall of Fame. Ingelsby, a 1973 Villanova alumnus, was one of the starting guards on Jack Kraft's 1971 team that lost to UCLA in the NCAA championship. He was named MVP of the Big 5 his senior year. In 1979, he was inducted into the Big 5 Hall of Fame.

Pinone, who received Academic All-America honors in 1982 and '83, was MVP of the Big 5 three consecutive years. He played for Rollie Massimino's 1983 team which won the Big 5 and played in the NCAA tournament.

Jensen, like Pinone, was a two-time Academic All-American. He played a key role in Villanova's big win

La Salle scholar Jack Hurd.

BIG 5 ACADEMIC ALL-AMERICANS
AND
NCAA GRADUATE SCHOLARS

Academic All-Americans

Bob Morse (Penn)
Tom Ingelsby (Villanova)
John Pinone (Villanova)
Harold Jensen (Villanova)
Tony DiLeo (La Salle)
Tim Legler (La Salle)
Jack Hurd (La Salle)

Post-graduate scholars

Charles McKenna (St. Joseph's)
Bob Morse (Penn)
Jack Hurd (La Salle)
John Pinone (Villanova)

over Georgetown for the 1985 NCAA championship. In 1986, Jensen received second-team All-Big 5 honors. A year ago, he was elected to the Big 5 Hall of Fame.

DiLeo, a 1978 La Salle graduate, played for Paul Westhead throughout his career with the Explorers. He played during the Michael Brooks Era at La Salle.

In 1978, he was a member of the Explorers' NCAA team which finished the season with an 18-12 record. Legler, a La Salle alumnus from the Class of 1988, played for Dave "Lefty" Ervin and Speedy Morris. He received All- Big 5 honors during his career. A year ago, he was inducted into the Big 5 Hall of Fame. Legler is currently playing for the Washington Bullets. Last season, he won the NBA's Long Distance Shootout at the All-Star game.

Hurd, a 1992 La Salle graduate, played on three NCAA tournament teams and one NIT team during his college career. He played for Speedy Morris and with three terrific players: Lionel Simmons, Doug Overton and Randy Woods. In 1992, he received first-team All-Big 5 honors. McKenna, a 1966 St. Joseph's graduate, is one of four Big 5 players to receive post-graduate honors. He played for Jack Ramsay's 1966 Hawk team, which finished the season with a 24-5 record and a third-place finish in the NIT. McKenna played with some marvelous players such as Matt Guokas, Cliff Anderson and Steve Courtin.

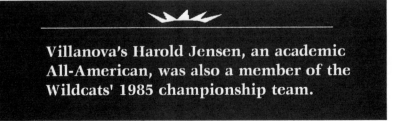

Villanova's Harold Jensen, an academic All-American, was also a member of the Wildcats' 1985 championship team.

THE BIG 5 HALL OF FAME

The first Big 5 Hall of Fame induction ceremony was February 1, 1973, at halftime of the Villanova-Notre Dame game at the Palestra. Each year, the Big 5 highlights some of the great players, coaches and others connected with the Big 5. This chapter provides a list of the Hall of Famers over the last 22 years.

1973
HALL OF FAMERS

CLIFFORD ANDERSON, ST. JOSEPH'S

LARRY CANNON, LA SALLE

WALI JONES, VILLANOVA

STAN PAWLAK, PENN

GUY RODGERS, TEMPLE

Larry Cannon was inducted into the Big 5 Hall of Fame in 1973.

1974 HALL OF FAMERS

FRANK CORACE, LA SALLE

HAL LEAR, TEMPLE

BOBBY McNEILL, ST.JOSEPH'S

BILL MELCHIONNI, VILLANOVA

JOHN WIDEMAN, PENN

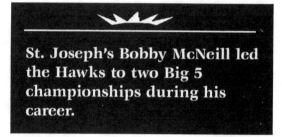

St. Joseph's Bobby McNeill led the Hawks to two Big 5 championships during his career.

Bill Melchionni, former Villanova star, played on the Philadelphia 76ers' 1966-67 NBA championship team.

(From left to right) Bill Kennedy (Temple,) Jim Lynam (St. Joseph's), Jim Washington (Villanova), John Rossiter (Original Big 5 manager), Jim Wolf (former Penn star accepting for Hall of Fame inductee Dave Wohl) and Ken Durrett (La Salle) were inducted into the Big 5 Hall of Fame in 1975. *Photo by Ed Mahan.*

1975 HALL OF FAMERS

KEN DURRETT, LA SALLE

BILL (PICKLES) KENNEDY, TEMPLE

JIM LYNAM, ST. JOSEPH'S

JOHN ROSSITER, ORIGINAL BIG 5 BUSINESS MANAGER

JIM WASHINGTON, VILLANOVA

DAVE WOHL, PENN

Jim Lynam, former St. Joseph's basketball star and coach, is currently the head coach of the Washington Bullets.

1976 HALL OF FAMERS

CORKY CALHOUN, PENN

MATT GUOKAS, ST. JOSEPH'S

BOB McATEER, LA SALLE

JAY NORMAN, TEMPLE

HUBIE WHITE, VILLANOVA

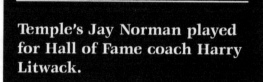

Temple's Jay Norman played for Hall of Fame coach Harry Litwack.

(From left to right), Matt Guokas, NBC color commentator, the late Irv Koslof, one-time owner of the Philadelphia 76ers, Alex Hannum, former 76ers head coach, Jack Ramsay, and Billy Cunningham, former head coach of the 76ers and part owner of the Miami Heat talk during a Big 5 Hall of Fame luncheon. *Photo by Ed Mahan.*

Chris Ford shared Big 5 MVP honors with Penn's Corky Calhoun in 1972.

Chris Ford led Villanova's 1971 team to the NCAA finals against UCLA.

1977 HALL OF FAMERS

BRUCE DRYSDALE, TEMPLE

CHRIS FORD, VILLANOVA

MIKE HAUER, ST. JOSEPH'S

HUBIE MARSHALL, LA SALLE

BOB MORSE, PENN

1978 HALL OF FAMERS

JOHN BAUM, TEMPLE

JIM HUGGARD, VILLANOVA

HARRY LITWACK, TEMPLE COACH

TOM WYNNE, ST. JOSEPH'S

Former Temple head coach Harry Litwack (center) was honored during a Big 5 Hall of Fame ceremony at the Palestra. Litwack was inducted into the Hall of Fame in 1978. He coached the 1969 Temple Owls to the NIT championship. He also coached the great backcourt combination of Guy Rodgers and Hal Lear. *Photo by Ed Mahan.*

(From left to right) John Baum (Temple), Jim Huggard (Villanova), Tom Wynne (St.Joseph's) and Harry Litwack (Temple) were inducted into the Big 5 Hall of Fame in 1978. *Photo by Ed Mahan.*

1979 HALL OF FAMERS

MIKE BANTOM, ST. JOSEPH'S

TOM INGELSBY, VILLANOVA

OLLIE JOHNSON, TEMPLE

Ollie Johnson, former Temple star, speaks during the Big 5 Hall of Fame luncheon in 1979. Johnson, an All-Big 5 performer, played several years in the NBA, including the Philadelphia 76ers. *Photo by Ed Mahan.*

Former Villanova athletic director Ted Aceto honors Tom Ingelsby during a Big 5 Hall of Fame ceremony at the Palestra in 1979. Ingelsby was voted MVP of the Big 5 in 1972. He is currently the men's head basketball coach of Archbishop Carroll High School in Radnor, Pennsylvania. *Photo by Ed Mahan.*

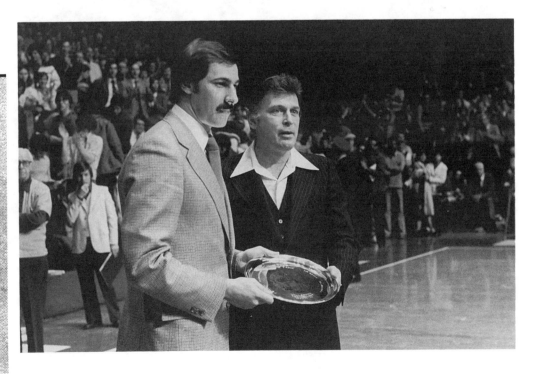

1980 HALL OF FAMERS

STEVE COURTIN, ST. JOSEPH'S

PHIL HANKINSON, PENN

DAN KELLY, ST. JOSEPH'S

ALONZO LEWIS, LA SALLE

La Salle's Alonzo Lewis is currently the head basketball coach at Cheyney University. Lewis received All-Big 5 honors in 1957.

(From left to right) Dan Kelly (St. Joseph's), Alonzo Lewis (La Salle), Phil Hankinson (Penn) and Steve Courtin (St. Joseph's) were inducted into the Big 5 Hall of Fame in 1980. *Photo by Ed Mahan.*

(From left to right) Charles Scott (Penn, assistant athletic director), Dick Censits (Penn) and Johnny Jones (Villanova) were honored during a Big 5 Hall of Fame ceremony at the Palestra in 1981. *Photo by Ed Mahan.*

Villanova's Johnny Jones was named MVP of the Big 5 in 1968.

1981 HALL OF FAMERS

JOE BRYANT, LA SALLE

DICK CENSITS, PENN

JOHNNY JONES, VILLANOVA

HOWARD PORTER, VILLANOVA

CHARLES SCOTT, PENN ASSISTANT ATHLETIC DIRECTOR

(From left to right) Johnny Jones (Villanova), Howard Porter (Villanova), Joe Bryant (La Salle), Dick Censits (Penn) and Charles Scott (Penn, assistant athletic director) were inducted into the Big 5 Hall of Fame in 1981. *Photo by Ed Mahan.*

Penn's Ron Haigler was named MVP of the Big 5 in 1974 and 1975.

1982 HALL OF FAMERS

ERNIE CASALE, TEMPLE ATHLETIC DIRECTOR

RON HAIGLER, PENN

BERNIE WILLIAMS, LA SALLE

CHARLIE WISE, LA SALLE

Charlie Wise averaged 16.7 points, shot 80.8% from the line and led the Big 5 in assists at 5.2. Wise had a career-high 29 vs. Villanova.

(From left to right) Former Philadelphia 76ers coaches Alex Hannum, Billy Cunningham and Jack Ramsay talk during a Big 5 Hall of Fame luncheon. *Photo by Ed Mahan.*

1983 HALL OF FAMERS

JACK RAMSAY, ST. JOSEPH'S COACH

JOE SPRATT, ST. JOSEPH'S

JOE STURGIS, PENN

JIM WILLIAMS, TEMPLE

(From left to right) Joe Sturgis (Penn), Joe Spratt (St. Joseph's) Jim Williams (Temple) and Don DiJulia (St. Joseph's athletic director accepting for Jack Ramsay) were inducted into the Big 5 Hall of Fame during a ceremony at the Palestra. *Photo by Ed Mahan.*

1984 HALL OF FAMERS

CLARENCE BROOKINS, TEMPLE

BOB FIELDS, LA SALLE

KEITH HERRON, VILLANOVA

PAT McFARLAND, ST. JOSEPH'S

JEFF NEUMAN, PENN

AL SHRIER, TEMPLE PUBLICIST

Bobby Fields led La Salle to a 20-7 record in 1971. Fields was a teammate of Ken Durrett, a two-time Big 5 MVP.

Al Meltzer (right), Channel 10 sports anchor and former play-by-play man for the Big 5 honors Villanova's Keith Herron (left) during a Big 5 Hall of Fame luncheon in 1984. Herron played four years in the NBA with Atlanta, Detroit and Cleveland.

1985 HALL OF FAMERS

NORMAN BLACK, ST. JOSEPH'S

KEVEN MCDONALD, PENN

JAKE NEVIN, VILLANOVA TRAINER

TONY PRICE, PENN

Former Penn athletic director Charles Harris (left) honors Keven McDonald (right) during a Big 5 Hall of Fame ceremony at the Spectrum. McDonald was inducted into the Big 5 Hall of Fame in 1985. The ex-Quaker was voted MVP of the Big 5 in 1977. *Photo by Ed Mahan.*

Former Penn athletic director Charles Harris (left) honors Tony Price (right) during a Big 5 Hall of Fame ceremony at the Spectrum. Price led the 1979 Quakers to the NCAA Final Four. *Photo by Ed Mahan.*

1986 HALL OF FAMERS

MICHAEL BROOKS, LA SALLE

KURT ENGELBERT, ST. JOSEPH'S

TOM GOLA, LA SALLE

RORY SPARROW, VILLANOVA

Tom Gola, former La Salle basketball coach and player, speaks during a Big 5 Hall of Fame luncheon. Gola coached the 1969 Explorers to a 23-1 record while capturing the Big 5 championship. *Photo by Ed Mahan.*

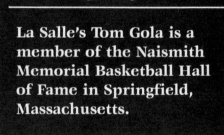

La Salle's Tom Gola is a member of the Naismith Memorial Basketball Hall of Fame in Springfield, Massachusetts.

Former La Salle athletic director Bill Bradshaw honors Tom Gola during a Big 5 Hall of Fame ceremony at the Palestra. *Photo by Ed Mahan.*

1987 HALL OF FAMERS

ALEX BRADLEY, VILLANOVA

TIM CLAXTON, TEMPLE

JACK KRAFT, VILLANOVA

MARCELLUS (BOO) WILLIAMS, ST. JOSEPH'S

Jack Kraft led Villanova to the 1971 NCAA Finals against the UCLA Bruins. The Wildcats lost to the Bruins, 68-62.

1988 HALL OF FAMERS

STEVE BILSKY, PENN

HANK SIEMIONTKOWSKI, VILLANOVA

BOB VETRONE, PUBLICIST,
WRITER, BROADCASTER

BRYAN WARRICK, ST. JOSEPH'S

Bob Vetrone speaks during a Big 5 Hall of Fame ceremony. Vetrone, a noted sports publicist, sportswriter and broadcaster, was inducted into the Hall of Fame in 1988. He is currently the assistant sports information director of La Salle University. *Photo by Ed Mahan.*

St. Joseph's Bryan Warrick (left) and Villanova's Alex Bradley (right) talk during the Big 5 Hall of Fame luncheon. *Photo by Ed Mahan.*

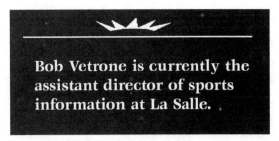

Bob Vetrone is currently the assistant director of sports information at La Salle.

St. Joseph's Bryan Warrick (left) and Villanova's Alex Bradley (right) reminisce during a Big 5 Hall of Fame luncheon.

Big 5 Hall of Fame "Cooperstown" picture (1989). Front row (left to right) Bob Bigelow (Penn), Keith Herron (Villanova), Bob Morse (Penn), Corky Calhoun (Penn), Joe Sturgis (Penn), Ron Haigler (Penn), Tom Gola (La Salle), Tom Ingelsby (Villanova) and Andy Dougherty (St. Joseph's). Back row (left to right) Alonzo Lewis (La Salle), Bob Vetrone (Big 5 publicist), Jay Norman (Temple), Dan Kelly (St. Joseph's), Frank Corace (La Salle), Bob McAteer (La Salle), Jim Williams (Temple), Bruce Drysdale (Temple), Jack Kraft (Villanova), Steve Courtin (St. Joseph's) and Al Meltzer (Channel 10 sports anchor). *Photo by Ed Mahan.*

1989 HALL OF FAMERS

BOB BIGELOW, PENN

ANDY DOUGHERTY, ST. JOSEPH'S PUBLICIST

JIM O'BRIEN, ST. JOSEPH'S

JOHN PINONE, VILLANOVA

BILLY TAYLOR, LA SALLE

Former Penn athletic director, now Executive Director of the Big 5, Paul Rubincam honors Quakers' basketball star Bob Bigelow during a Big 5 Hall of Fame ceremony at the Palestra. Bigelow was inducted into the Hall of Fame in 1989.

Terence Stansbury hit a last-second shot to beat St. John's 65-63 in the NCAA tournament in 1984.

Former Penn athletic director, now Executive Director of the Big 5, Paul Rubincam (right) honors Bob McKee (left) during a Big 5 Hall of Fame ceremony at the Palestra. McKee, a long-time scorer for the Big 5, was inducted into the Hall of Fame in 1990. *Photo by Ed Mahan.*

Al Meltzer (right), Channel 10 sports anchor, honors Temple's Granger Hall during a Big 5 luncheon. Ed Pinckney (lower left) is also shown. *Photo by Ed Mahan.*

1991 HALL OF FAMERS

GRANGER HALL, TEMPLE

RALPH LEWIS, LA SALLE

ED PINCKNEY, VILLANOVA

JOE RYAN, VILLANOVA

Villanova's Ed Pinckney speaks during a Big 5 Hall of Fame induction ceremony. Pinckney was inducted into the Hall of Fame in 1991. *Photo by Ed Mahan.*

La Salle's Ralph Lewis was named MVP of the Big 5 in 1984.

La Salle's Ralph Lewis speaks during a Big 5 Hall of Fame luncheon. Lewis was inducted in 1991. *Photo by Ed Mahan.*

Harold Pressley is the Villanova career steals leader with 218 in his career from 1982-86.

1992 HALL OF FAMERS

STEVE BLACK, LA SALLE

MAURICE MARTIN, ST. JOSEPH'S

JACK MCKINNEY, ST. JOSEPH'S

HAROLD PRESSLEY, VILLANOVA

Former Penn head coach Dick Harter speaks during a Big 5 Hall of Fame luncheon; he was inducted in 1993. Harter is currently an assistant coach of the Portland Trail Blazers. *Photo by Ed Mahan.*

1993 HALL OF FAMERS

NATE BLACKWELL, TEMPLE

JIM CRAWFORD, LA SALLE

DICK HARTER, PENN COACH

AL MELTZER, BIG 5 TV ANNOUNCER

DWAYNE MCCLAIN, VILLANOVA

Nate Blackwell, former Temple All-American, is currently an assistant coach with the Owls' basketball team.

Al Meltzer speaks during a Big 5 Hall of Fame luncheon. Meltzer, former television play-by-play man, was inducted into the Hall of Fame in 1993. He is currently the sports anchor for Channel 10 in Philadelphia. *Photo by Ed Mahan.*

1994 HALL OF FAMERS

RODNEY BLAKE, ST. JOSEPH'S

HOWARD EVANS, TEMPLE

JACK MCCLOSKEY, PENN

TIM PERRY, TEMPLE

AL SEVERANCE, VILLANOVA COACH

Howard Evans played in the backcourt with Mark Macon on Temple's 1987-88 team that was ranked No. 1 in the country.

St. Joseph's
Rodney Blake

1995 HALL OF FAMERS

HAROLD JENSEN, VILLANOVA

TIM LEGLER, LA SALLE

JOHN ENGLES, PENN

MIKE VREESWYK, TEMPLE

HARVEY POLLACK, BIG 5 STATISTICIAN

Temple's Mike Vreeswyk was a 1987-88 starter for the Owls. He was one of the most prolific long-distance shooters in school history.

Temple's MikeVreeswyk led the Owls to an NIT appearance in 1989.

Villanova's Doug West.

Doug West is third on
Villanova's scoring list with
2,026 points and a 22.8 average
during his career from 1985-89.

1996 HALL OF FAMERS

LIONEL SIMMONS, LA SALLE
DOUG WEST, VILLANOVA
JEFFERY CLARK, ST. JOSEPH'S

St. Joseph's Jeffery Clark
tied for Big 5 MVP honors
with Villanova's John
Pinone in 1982.

THE BIG 5 FROM A TO Z
AND BY THE NUMBERS

B ob Vetrone Jr., a sports copy editor of the *Philadelphia Daily News*, published his version of some of the things that happened in the history of the Big 5 and at the Palestra over the last 40 years. Here's an A to Z story of Philadelphia college basketball along with some great Big 5 moments and accomplishments. This article is reprinted with permission of Bob Vetrone and *The Philadelphia Daily News*.

A is for Anthony Arnolie, who made 10 consecutive free throws in the final 2:29 to lead Penn over ninth-ranked Villanova, 84-80 (December 11, 1982).

B is for Jim Boyle, who nailed the game-winner from the foul line to give St. Joseph's a 58-57 shocker over top-ranked Bowling Green, in the first round of the Quaker City Tournament (December 26, 1962).

C is for Calvin Murphy, who, in his fifth collegiate game, poured in a still-standing Palestra record of 52 points in Niagara's 100-83 win over La Salle (December 16, 1967).

Bob Vetrone Sr., long-time publicist, sportswriter and sportscaster, was inducted into the Big 5 Hall of Fame in 1988. Vetrone is currently the assistant director of sports information at La Salle.

Although Steve Donches does not rank personally among the top ten leaders in scoring, this basket certainly does. Donches, a reserve guard, nailed this dramatic buzzer-beater to defeat Villanova, 71-69 on January 16, 1966.

D is for Steve Donches, who nailed a 29-footer from the corner to give St. Joseph's a 71-69 win over Villanova (January 16, 1966).

E is for Eric Erickson, who scored off a backdoor pass from Wali Jones with four seconds left in overtime to lift Villanova over St. Joseph's, 63-61 (January 12, 1963).

F is for Bobby Fields, who scored 30 points as La Salle, without injured All-America Ken Durrett, surprised Villanova, 73-69 (February 13, 1971).

G is for Tom Garberina, whose tip-in at the end of the second overtime forced a third extra period to set up La Salle's 111-105 win over Villanova (January 11, 1958).

H is for Hal Lear, who, suffering from the flu, made a pair of free throws with two seconds left to give Temple a 60-58 win over Canisius in the NCAA Eastern Regional Final (March 17, 1956).

Villanova's Tom Ingelsby (24) plays defense during a non-conference game against Philadelphia Textile at the Palestra. Ingelsby was named MVP of the Big 5 in 1973. *Photo by Ed Mahan.*

I is for Tom Ingelsby, who scored 28 points—including the two free throws with six seconds left — that decided Villanova's 77-76 win over third-ranked South Carolina in the Quaker City Tournament final (December 30, 1971).

Tom Ingelsby, Big 5 MVP, had an excellent season, averaging 25.5 points for Villanova. He also became the fifth player to score 100 points in a Big 5 season.

J is for Jim McDaniels, whose fifth-ranked Western Kentucky team fell to Ken Durrett (45 points, 14 rebounds) and La Salle, 91-76 (January 16, 1971).

K is for Les Keiter, who remained high atop the Palestra continuing his telecast as the rest of the building was evacuated during a bomb scare at halftime of St. Joseph's 69-61 win over Villanova (February 20, 1965).

St. Joseph's coach Jim Lynam.

L is for the Lynams. St. Joseph's Jimmy had the assist on the game-winner over Bowling Green in '62. Kevin nailed the game-winner in La Salle's 84-83 triple overtime win over Villanova (December 20, 1980).

M is for Mascot, as in St. Joseph's Hawk, who was ambushed by the La Salle male cheerleaders during a second-half timeout in the Hawks' 73-63 victory over the Explorers (January 19, 1988).

N is for Navy, which was stunned as Drexel overcame a 17-4 deficit and a 44-point, 14-rebound performance by David Robinson to upset the 18th-ranked Midshipmen, 83-80 (January 21, 1987).

O is for Oscar Robertson, who scored 43 points as a sophomore in Cincinnati's 100-78 victory over St. Joseph's (February 8, 1958).

St. Joseph's Hawk mascot spreads his wings during a timeout at the Palestra. *Photo by Ed Mahan.*

St. Joseph's Hawk mascot made its debut on January 4, 1956, a 69-56 win over La Salle at the Palestra. Since then, 19 other St. Joe's students have donned the suit.

P is for Ed Pinckney, who brought the big house down twice in 10 days. He avoided a charge and nailed a baseline jumper with one second left to give Villanova a 72-71 win over La Salle (Jan. 22, 1983). He followed that up with a 27-point, 22-rebound performance as the Wildcats overcame a 14-point deficit and beat Georgetown, 68-67 (January 31, 1983).

Q is for the 1961 Quaker City Tournament, won by St. Joseph's, 76-69, over second-ranked Wichita State (December 29, 1964). After the game, Shockers coach Gary Thompson said he never would bring another team of his back to the Palestra.

R is for Rollouts, often tasteless, always hilarious.

S is for Sixty Minutes, which is how long it took Providence to top Villanova, 90-83, in a four-overtime thriller (January 24, 1959).

T is for twenty-four, as in 24-0, which is how Temple opened its 84-50 win over Penn (January 6, 1989).

U is for Upsets, Two more that stand out: St. Joseph's, after trailing, 10-0 dismantled second-ranked De Paul, 58-45 (February 7, 1984); and Penn's 71-70 win over 17th-ranked Villanova (December 6, 1988).

V is for Big 5 Hall of Famer Bob Vetrone Sr.

W is for Wilt Chamberlain (Kansas) and Jerry West (West Virginia), who joined Cincinnati's Oscar Robertson on the 1957-58 all-opponents team.

X is for X, the Roman numeral for 10, which is the number of games played each year in the City Series when it was a full round-robin. Which also makes it X for X-tinct.

Y is for Yo-Yo. And if you have to ask, you shouldn't have read this far.

Z is for zzzz. Penn 32, Villanova 30 (January 15, 1969).

THE BIG 5 BY THE NUMBERS

1 is where Villanova ended the 1984-85 season after beating Georgetown, 66-64, for the NCAA championship.

2 is for Temple, who knocked off two top five teams in the same week. In 1995, the Owls defeated then No.-1 ranked Kansas and No. 2-ranked Villanova.

3 is for Temple's Guy Rodgers, Villanova's John Pinone, La Salle's Ken Durrett and Lionel Simmons, who were all three-time MVPs of the Big 5.

4 is for Cliff Anderson who finished fourth on St. Joseph's all-time scoring list with 1,728 points.

5 is for Joe Sturgis who finished with the fifth-highest career scoring average (17.5 ppg) in Penn's basketball history.

6 is for Temple's margin of victory over La Salle, 63-57 in 1961.

7 is for Kareem Townes, a high-scoring guard, who finished his career at No. 7 on the Explorers' all-time steals list.

8 is the number of field goals La Salle's Albert "Truck" Butts made in his team's 96-85 victory over Penn in 1984.

9 is for Don Casey, who coached the Temple Owls for nine seasons (1973-82).

10 is the number of players chosen for the 1956-57 All-Big 5 team: Mel Brodsky, Temple; Dick Censits, Penn; Dan Dougherty, St. Joseph's; Kurt Engelbert, St. Joseph's; Tom Garberina, La Salle, Al Griffith, Villanova; Alonzo Lewis, La Salle; Jay Norman, Temple, Ray Radziszewski, St. Joseph's; and Guy Rodgers, Temple.

11 is for Boo Williams, who shot 11-for-11 from the free throw line in St. Joseph's 60-56 three-overtime victory over Penn in 1980.

12 is the number of assists Penn's John Wilson dished out against Princeton in 1986.

13 is the number of home games Villanova played at the John E. duPont Pavilion in 1989.

14 is for Penn, who posted a 14-0 Ivy League record in 1995.

15 is the number of seasons John Chaney has coached at Temple.

16 is for Villanova's Jim Huggard and Fran O'Hanlon, who both handed out a school-record 16 assists in one game.

17 is for Tim Perry, who had 17 rebounds against St. Joseph's at McGonigle Hall.

18 is the number of rebounds Michael Brooks pulled down in La Salle's 82-74 win over St. Joseph's in 1978.

19 is the number of free throws attempted by Temple's Granger Hall in a Big 5 contest against Villanova in 1983.

20 is for Steve Black, who as a freshman was one of the country's highest freshman scorers averaging 20 points a game.

21 is for Penn's Ron Haigler, Stan Pawlak and Keven McDonald, who all had respective career scoring averages of 21.6, 21.5 and 21.2.

22 is the number of games the NIT champion Temple Owls (22-8) won in 1969.

23 is for Tim Claxton, who scored 23 points to lead Temple to a 87-75 win over La Salle at the Palestra in 1977.

24 is for Wali Jones, who wore jersey No. 24 throughout his career at Villanova.

25 is for Chuck Daly, who won 25 games in his first year as the Quakers' head coach in 1971-72. Penn's overall record was 25-3.

WOMEN IN THE BIG 5

M ainly due to the success of the local men's college basketball teams, the Philadelphia Big 5 schools decided to expand the round robin play to crown a City Series champion for the women in 1979. Although the teams had established this format in 1973-74, the development of the women's Big 5 program didn't occur until 1989, when four of the five teams participated in the NCAA tournament.

Carolyn Schlie Femovich, senior associate athletic director at the University of Pennsylvania, who was the chairperson of the Women's Big 5, announced that Dan Baker, former Big 5 Executive Director, would be responsible for organizing radio and television coverage, postseason luncheons and dinners and the Women's Big 5 Hall of Fame.

This format has contributed to the increasing popularity of women's college basketball in Philadelphia. The Big 5 has produced some tremendous women basketball players such as St. Joseph's Dale Hodges, Temple's Marilyn Stephens, Villanova's Shelly Pennefather, La Salle's Jennifer Cole and Penn's Kirsten Brendel.

St. Joseph's Dale Hodges.

Dale Hodges is one of the top scoring women in Big 5 history, despite playing just three seasons.

Entering his 11th season, La Salle women's head basketball coach John Miller has compiled a 204-89 record, and has been named Big 5 Coach of the Year three times.

Hodges finished her career with 2,077 points and put together two magnificent season point totals in Big 5, scoring 725 points as a junior and 855 as a senior. She set a school record 42 points against Temple. Hodges is a member of the Women's Big 5 Hall of Fame.

Stephens was the first women's Big 5 player to score 30 points in a City Series game. She scored 37 points in a 116-66 win over La Salle in 1984 at Temple's McGonigle Hall. Stephens is a member of the Women's Big 5 Hall of Fame.

Pennefather, a Big 5 Hall of Famer, was the first woman to receive the Big 5 Player of the Year award three consecutive years (1985, 1986, 1987). She completed her career scoring 2,408 points.

Cole led the Explorers to a 25-8 record which included a Big 5 title in 1992. She averaged 20.8 points while shooting 87 percent from the free throw line. She was also named the Big 5's Most Valuable Player that same year.

Brendel played a key role in helping the Quakers post a winning record in 1991 with a 15-11 mark. She averaged 24.3 points and 11 rebounds. Brendel won Big 5 Player of the Year honors and her coach Julie Soriero was named Coach of the Year.

In the 1979-80 season, the first official year for the Big 5 women's teams, Villanova's Lisa Ortlip was named MVP. As a sophomore, Ortlip helped guide the Wildcats to the first Big 5 championship and averaged 14.4 points for the 20-5 Villanova team.

Quakers coach Julie Soriero, in her 17th season of coaching college basketball, is the chairperson of the Ivy League Women's Basketball Coaches Association.

There are many other players who had outstanding Big 5 careers such as St. Joseph's Debbie Black, Muffet O'Brien, Mary Sue Garrity, Chrissy McGoldrick, Renie Dunn, Trish Brown, Terri Mohr, Teresa Carmichael and Kim Foley; Temple's Faye Lawrence, Lynn Blaszczyk, Donna Kennedy, Mimi Carroll, Theresa Govens, Addie Jackson and Pam Balogh; Penn's Carol Kuna, Vivian Machinski, Sharon Gross, Auretha Fleming, Barbara Albom, Beth Stegner and Sandy Hawthorne; La Salle's Maureen Kramer, Ellen Malone, Julie Reidenauer, Kathy Bess, Linda Hester and Suzi McCaffrey; Villanova's Lisa Ortlip, Kathy Straccia, Karen Hiznay, Stephanie Vanderslice, Kathy Beisel, Nancy Bernhardt and Lisa Angelotti.

In the first official season of Big 5 play, first-team honors went to: Kathy Bess (La Salle), Lynn Blaszczyk (Temple), Renie Dunne (St Joseph's), Joanne Gentry (St Joseph's) and Lisa Ortlip, MVP (Villanova).

Villanova Women's Head Basketball Coach Harry Perretta, in his 19th season has had great success leading the Wildcats, compiling a 333-183 record.

In terms of coaching, Jim Foster, former St. Joseph's head coach who is now the head man at Vanderbilt, is one of the most successful coaches in the history of the women's Big 5. Foster won six Big 5 championships from 1979 to 1991. During those years, he guided the Lady Hawks to six NCAA tournament appearances.

Linda McDonald, ex-Temple coach who is now the head basketball coach at Minnesota, had several winning seasons for the Lady Owls. Presently, the most successful coaches in the Big 5 are La Salle's John Miller (204-89), Villanova's Harry Perretta (333-183) and St. Joseph's Stephanie Gaitley (209-113). While the others have achieved great success, Penn's Julie Soriero (191-204) and Temple's Kristen Foley (35-102) have taken some positive steps in rebuilding their programs.

TOP FIVE POINT SCORERS IN A SINGLE GAME

Player (School)	Opponent/Date	FG	FT	Pts.
1. Marilyn Stephens (Temple)	La Salle/1-7-84	13	11	37
Jenn Cole (La Salle)	Penn/11-30-91	10	15	37
3. Kirsten Brendel (Penn)	St.Joseph's/1-16-90	11	13	35
4. Addie Jackson (Temple)	Penn/2-23-88	12	1	30
5. Marilyn Stephens (Temple)	Penn/2-5-83	11	7	29

SOME OF THE BIG 5's OUTSTANDING WOMEN

La Salle's Jennifer Cole led the Explorers to 25 wins by averaging 20.8 points while shooting 87 percent from the line and 41 percent from three-point range.

Penn's Kirsten Brendel, '91 Big 5 MVP (above), had an amazing season, averaging 24.3 points and 11.0 boards. She became the first woman to score 100 points in a Big 5 season.

All-American, two-year Big 5 MVP ('89 and '90), Dale Hodges (left) averaged a Big 5 all-time high of 27.6 points a game for St. Joe, which included three games of more than 40 points.

Villanova's Shelly Pennefather (below), three-time Big 5 MVP ('85, '86, '87), won the Margaret Wade Trophy and scored 272 points in 16 Big 5 games in her career. She is the only woman ever to be chosen Big 5 MVP three times.

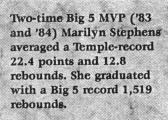

Two-time Big 5 MVP ('83 and '84) Marilyn Stephens averaged a Temple-record 22.4 points and 12.8 rebounds. She graduated with a Big 5 record 1,519 rebounds.

BIG 5 PLAYERS IN THE PROS

For more than 40 years, the Big 5 has sent great players to the NBA. The Big 5 has also produced several players who spent a few seasons in the old ABA. This chapter highlights players who have gone on to the professional ranks from La Salle, Penn, St. Joseph's, Temple, and Villanova.

LA SALLE UNIVERSITY EXPLORERS

Bernie Williams
San Diego Rockets ('69-71)
Virginia Squires ('71-74).

Roland (Fatty) Taylor
Washington Bullets ('69-70),
Virginia Squires ('70-74 & '75-76)
Denver Nuggets ('74-75 & '76-77).

George Sutor
Kentucky Colonels/Minnesota ('68-69),
Carolina Cougars/Miami Floridians ('69-70).

Tom Piotrowski
Portland Trail Blazers ('83-84).

Doug Overton
Washington Bullets ('92-95). He spent most of last season with the Denver Nuggets.

When Randy Woods was selected as the 16th selection in the '92 NBA draft by the LA Clippers, La Salle became one of only five schools to have at least one player drafted in each of the first three years of the NBA's two-round draft.

TIM LEGLER

Phoenix Suns ('89-90), Denver Nuggets ('90-91), Dallas Mavericks ('93-94), Golden State Warriors ('94-95). **Legler currently plays for the Washington Bullets.**

Ralph Lewis
Detroit Pistons ('87-90), Charlotte Hornets ('88-90).

Ken Durrett
Cincinnati Royals ('71-72),
Kansas City Omaha Kings ('72-75),
Philadelphia 76ers ('74-75).

Bob Fields
Utah Stars ('71-72).

Larry Cannon
Miami Floridians ('69-70),
Denver Nuggets ('70-71),
Memphis Pros ('71-72),
Indiana Pacers ('71-74),
Philadelphia 76ers ('73-74).

Tim Legler owns the La Salle record for percentage of three-pointers made in a season: 49.1% (104-212) in 34 games, in 1987-88.

Three La Salle draftees—Tom Gola (1954), Michael Brooks (1980) and Lionel Simmons (1990)—were also honored as NCAA Players of the year.

Michael Brooks
San Diego Clippers ('80-84),
Indiana Pacers ('86-87),
Denver Nuggets ('87-88).

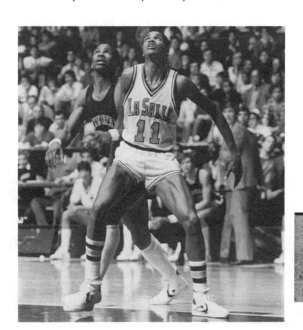

Ralph Lewis blocks out around the basket. Lewis played on the Detroit Pistons' 1988-89 team that lost to the Los Angeles Lakers for the NBA championship.

La Salle's Larry Cannon is 12th in career scoring average with 19.1 from 1966-69.

A three-time collegiate All-American, Tom Gola played for the Philadelphia Warriors and New York Knicks and was named All-Pro five times.

Joe Bryant
Philadelphia 76ers ('75-79), San Diego Clippers ('79-82), Houston Rockets (82-83).

Joe Bryant was La Salle's 1974-75 scoring leader with 632 points, a 21.8 average.

Lionel Simmons is La Salle's all-time leading scorer, the third leading scorer in NCAA history, and the only player to score over 3,000 points and pull down 1,429 rebounds.

LIONEL SIMMONS

Lionel Simmons is currently in the NBA playing for the Sacramento Kings ('90-96).

Randy Woods
Los Angeles Clippers ('92-95).
Woods was released by the Denver Nuggets in 1996.

UNIVERSITY OF PENNSYLVANIA

Jerome Allen
Played for the Minnesota Timberwolves during the 1995-96 season.

Bob Bigelow
Kansas City Omaha Kings ('75-77),
Boston Celtics ('77-78),
San Diego Clippers ('78-79).

Corky Calhoun
Phoenix Suns ('72-75),
Los Angeles Lakers ('74-76),
Portland Trail Blazers ('76-78),
Indiana Pacers ('78-80).

Phil Hankinson
Boston Celtics ('73-75).

Phil Hankinson was Penn's 1972-73 scoring leader with 512 points, and a 18.3 average.

Dave Wohl
Philadelphia 76ers ('71-72),
Portland Trail Blazers ('72-73),
Buffalo Braves ('72-74),
Houston Rockets ('73-77),
New York Nets ('76-78).

Tony Price
San Diego Clippers (80-81).

Penn's Dave Wohl was the second-leading scorer (15.3 ppg) on the Quakers' 1979-71 28-1 team. Wohl played and coached in the NBA. He is currently vice president of basketball operations with the Miami Heat.

THE PHILADELPHIA BIG 5

ST. JOSEPH'S UNIVERSITY

Cliff Anderson
Los Angeles Lakers ('67-69),
Denver Nuggets ('69-70),
Cleveland Cavaliers/Philadelphia 76ers ('70-71)

Mike Bantom
Phoenix Suns (73-75),
Seattle SuperSonics (75-76),
New York Nets (76-77),
Indiana Pacers (77-81),
Philadelphia 76ers (81-82).

Norman Black
Detroit Pistons ('80-81).

Steve Courtin
Philadelphia 76ers ('64-65).

Bill DeAngelis
New York Nets ('70-71).

Matt Guokas is seventh on St. Joe's all-time assists list, with 155 in 1964-65.

The only Olympian in St. Joe's men's basketball history, Mike Bantom is one of just four Hawk players to compile over 1,000 points and rebounds in a career. Currently an executive with the NBA after a stellar ten-year career in the league, Bantom still ranks seventh on the SJU all-time scoring list with 1,684 points and second on the rebound chart with 1,151 caroms.

Matt Guokas
Philadelphia 76ers ('66-71),
Chicago Bulls ('70-71 & '74-76),
Cincinnati ('71-72),
Kansas City Omaha Kings ('72-74 & '75-76),
Houston Rockets/Buffalo Braves ('73-74).

Maurice Martin
Denver Nuggets ('86-88).

Pat McFarland
Denver Nuggets ('73-75),
San Diego Clippers ('75-76).

Bobby McNeill
New York Knicks ('60-61),
Philadelphia 76ers/Los Angeles Lakers
('61-62).

Ray Radziszewski
Philadelphia Warriors ('57-58).

Bryan Warrick
Washington Bullets ('82-84),
Los Angeles Clippers ('84-85),
Milwaukee Bucks/Indiana Pacers ('85-86).

Matt Guokas was a member of the "Mighty Mites," so dubbed because of their noticeable lack of size. These legends in Hawk lore led SJU to a combined 54-15 mark over a four-year period, making up for their lack of height with quick passing, smothering defense, and an assortment of gadget plays.

St. Joseph's Jack McKinney

SJU IN THE NBA

Six St. Joseph players have gone on to head coaching careers in the NBA

Jack Ramsay

Jack McKinney

Paul Westhead

Jim Lynam

Matt Guokas

George Senesky

TEMPLE UNIVERSITY

John Baum
Chicago Bulls ('69-71),
New York Nets ('71-73),
Memphis Pros/Indiana Pacers ('73-74).

Nate Blackwell
San Antonio ('87-88).

Clarence Brookins
Miami Floridians ('70-71).

DUANE CAUSWELL

Sacramento Kings ('90-96)

Duane Causwell was the 18th pick in the first round of the NBA draft and went to Sacramento.

Donald Hodge
Dallas Mavericks ('91-95).
Hodge was released by the Mavericks in 1996.

Donald Hodge was the leader in field goal percentage for Temple in 1989-90 (54.1) and 1990-91 (53.5%).

Ollie Johnson
Portland Trail Blazers ('72-74),
New Orleans Jazz ('74-75),
Kansas City Omaha Kings ('74-77),
Atlanta Hawks ('77-78),
Chicago Bulls ('78-80),
Philadelphia 76ers ('80-82).

EDDIE JONES

Former Temple star Eddie Jones is in his third year with the Los Angeles Lakers.

Eddie Jones was a member of the 1995 NBA all-rookie team. Jones was the first Laker rookie to score in double figures since Magic Johnson.

Bill Kennedy
Philadelphia Warriors ('60-61).

Hal Lear
Philadelphia Warriors ('56-57).

Mark Macon
Denver Nuggets ('91-93),
Denver/Detroit Pistons ('93-94),
Detroit ('94-95).
Macon was released by the
Pistons in 1996.

Ed Mast
New York Knicks ('70-72),
Atlanta Hawks ('72-73).

AARON McKIE

Portland Trail Blazers ('94-96).

Mark Macon led all Temple scorers for
four years, from 1988-89 to 1990-91.

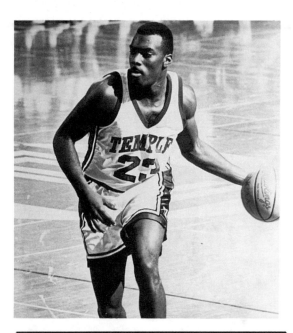

Aaron McKie had the highest free throw
percentage in three years, '91-92 (75.4), '92-
93 (78.9), and '93-94 (81.6).

TIM PERRY

Phoenix Suns ('88-92),
Philadelphia 76ers ('92-95).
Perry was traded to the New Jersey Nets
in 1996.

Eddie Jones and Aaron McKie became
the first pair of Owls ever to be
chosen in the first round of the NBA
draft in the same year. They also
became the first teammates in the
history of the Big 5 and the Atlantic
10 Conference to be selected in the
first round in the same year.

In the first season of the formal Big 5, the Philadelphia Warriors had seven players who had played at Big 5 schools: Paul Arizin, Ernie Beck, Jack George, Tom Gola, Larry Hennessy, Jackie Moore and Bob Schafer.

Ramon Rivas
Boston Celtics ('88-89).

Guy Rodgers
Philadelphia/San Warriors ('58-66),
Chicago Bulls ('66-68),
Cincinnati Royals ('67-68),
Milwaukee Bucks ('68-70).

Terence Stansbury
Indiana Pacers ('84-86),
Seattle SuperSonics ('86-87).

VILLANOVA UNIVERSITY

Alex Bradley
New York Knicks ('81-82).

Chris Ford
Detroit Pistons ('72-79),
Boston Celtics
('78-82).

Stewart Granger
Cleveland Cavaliers ('83-84),
Atlanta Hawks ('84-85),
New York Knicks ('86-87).

Keith Herron
Atlanta Hawks ('78-79),
Detroit Pistons ('80-81),
Cleveland Cavaliers ('81-82).

Tom Hoover
New York Knicks ('63-65),
St. Louis Hawks ('66-67),
Denver Nuggets ('67-68),
Houston Rockets, Minnesota,
New York Knicks ('68-69).

Tom Ingelsby
Atlanta Hawks ('73-74),
St. Louis Spirit ('74-75),
San Diego Clippers ('75-76).

Stewart Granger was a Big East All-Tournament honoree in 1983.

Villanova has retired the jerseys of former Wildcat greats including: Paul Arizin, Wali Jones, Bill Melchionni, Jake Nevin, Shelly Pennefather, and Al Severance.

KERRY KITTLES

New Jersey Nets ('96-97)

Wali Jones
Baltimore Bullets ('64-65),
Philadelphia 76ers ('65-71),
Milwaukee Bucks ('71-73),
Utah Stars ('74-75),
Detroit Pistons/Philadelphia 76ers ('75-76).

Dwayne McClain
Indiana Pacers ('85-86).

Bill Melchionni
Philadelphia 76ers ('66-68),
New York Nets ('69-75).

Fran O'Hanlon
Miami Floridians ('70-71).

John Olive
San Diego Clippers ('78-80).

Ed Pinckney
Phoenix Suns ('85-87),
Sacramento Kings ('87-89),
Boston Celtics ('88-94),
Milwaukee Bucks ('94-95),
Toronto Raptors ('95-96),
Philadelphia 76ers ('95-96).
Miami Heat ('96-97)

Ed Pinckney goes up for two points against Temple in a Big 5 game at the Palestra.

John Pinone
Atlanta Hawks ('83-84).

Howard Porter
Chicago Bulls ('71-74),
New York Knicks ('74-75),
Detroit Pistons ('74-78),
New Jersey Nets ('77-78).

Harold Pressley
Sacramento Kings ('86-90).

Rory Sparrow
New Jersey Nets ('80-81),
Atlanta Hawks ('81-83),
New York Knicks ('82-88),
Chicago Bulls ('87-88),
Miami Heat ('90-91),
Sacramento Kings ('90-91),
Chicago Bulls/Los Angeles Lakers ('91-92).

Jim Washington
St. Louis Hawks ('65-66),
Chicago Bulls ('66-69),
Philadelphia 76ers ('69-72),
Atlanta Hawks ('71-75),
Buffalo Braves ('74-75).

Penn's Tyrone Pitts and Villanova's Harold Pressley battle it out at the Palestra.

DOUG WEST

Minnesota Timberwolves ('89-96).

Hubie White
San Francisco Warriors ('62-63),
Philadelphia 76ers ('63-64),
Miami Floridians ('69-70),
Pittsburgh Condors ('70-71).

Doug West played at Villanova from 1985-89, finishing his career as the Wildcats' third-leading scorer. Since his graduation, he has established himself as a key player for the Minnesota Timberwolves.

APPENDICES

LA SALLE RECORDS

ALL-TIME LEADING SCORERS

Lionel Simmons, 3,217
Michael Brooks, 2,628
Tom Gola, 2,461
Steve Black, 2,021
Kareem Townes, 1,925
Randy Woods, 1,811
Ralph Lewis, 1,807
Doug Overton, 1,795
Tim Legler, 1,699
Jack Hurd, 1,693
Ken Durrett, 1,679
Hubie Marshall, 1,576
Billy Taylor, 1,554
Larry Foust, 1,464
Larry Cannon, 1,430
Frank Corace, 1,411
Larry Koretz, 1,382
Paul Burke, 1,368
Kurt Kanaskie, 1,356
Charlie Wise, 1,245
Norm Grekin, 1,243
Mo Connolly, 1,232
Bernie Williams, 1,230
Chip Greenberg, 1,227
Jim Crawford, 1,213
Fred Lehle, 1,204
Bob Walters, 1,193
Craig Conlin, 1,159
Alonzo Lewis, 1,137
Donn Wilber, 1,127
Joe Bryant, 1,118
Romaine Haywood, 1,083
Albert Butts, 1,060
Bob McAteer, 1,056
George Paull, 1,016
Bob Fields, 1,016
Rich Tarr, 1,004

MOST CAREER REBOUNDS

Tom Gola, 2,201
Lionel Simmons, 1,429
Michael Brooks, 1,372
Ralph Lewis, 966
Ken Durrett, 850
Norm Grekin, 832
George Sutor, 826
Walter Sampson, 791
Bob Alden, 784
Albert Butts, 780
Jim Wolkiewicz, 773
Milko Lieverst, 751

MOST CAREER BLOCKED SHOTS

Lionel Simmons, 248
Ron Barnes, 107
Ralph Lewis, 94
Tom Piotrowski, 67
Albert Butts, 63

MOST CAREER ASSISTS

Doug Overton, 671
Paul Burke, 567
Darryl Gladden, 461
Chip Greenberg, 461
Rich Tarr, 429
Charlie Wise, 407
Greg Webster, 368
Kurt Kanaskie, 366
Lionel Simmons, 355
Larry Cannon, 347
Randy Woods, 340
Glenn Collier, 278
Kevin Lynam, 261
Tim Legler, 244

MOST CAREER STEALS

Doug Overton, 277
Lionel Simmons, 239
Randy Woods, 220
Paul Burke, 214
Jack Hurd, 205
Ralph Lewis, 200
Kareem Townes, 196
Chip Greenberg, 176
Rich Tarr, 134

Steve Black, 118
Tim Legler, 112
Dallas Philson, 106
Larry Koretz, 84
Albert Butts, 82
Craig Conlin, 78
Peter Tiano, 71

ALL-TIME COACHING RECORDS

- Bill "Speedy" Morris, 1986-1996, 10 years, 183-119
- Dave "Lefty" Ervin, 1979-1986, 7 years, 119-87
- Paul Westhead, 1970-1979, 9 years, 142-105
- Tom Gola, 1968-1970, 2 years, 37-13
- Jim Harding, 1967-1968, 1 year, 20-8
- Joe Heyer, 1965-1967, 2 years, 24-27
- Bob Walters, 1963-1965, 2 years, 31-17
- Donald "Dudey" Moore, 1958-1963, 5 years, 79-37
- Jim Pollard, 1955-1958, 3 years, 48-28
- Ken Loeffler, 1949-1955, 6 years, 145-30
- Charles McGlone, 1946-1949, 3 years, 61-17
- Joseph Meehan, 1943-1946, 3 years, 28-30
- Charles "Obie" O'Brien, 1941-1943, 2 years, 25-21
- Leonard Tanser, 1933-1941, 8 years, 90-59
- Thomas Conley, 1931-1933, 2 years, 28-11
- James J. Henry, 1930-1931, 1 year, 15-4

PENNSYLVANIA RECORDS

ALL-TIME LEADING SCORERS

Ernie Beck, 1,827
Keven McDonald, 1,644
Ron Haigler, 1,552
Jerome Allen, 1,518
Stan Pawlak, 1,501
Bruce Lefkowitz, 1,443
Matt Maloney, 1,370
Herb Lyon, 1,333
Tony Price, 1,322
Tyrone Pitts, 1,301
Joe Sturgis, 1,292
Perry Bromwell, 1,265
Barry Pierce, 1,245
Phil Hankinson, 1,236
Dave Wohl, 1,226
Richard Censits, 1,220
Jeff Neuman, 1,187
Paul Little, 1,116
Steve Bilsky, 1,108
Richard Heylmun, 1,076
Corky Calhoun, 1,066
John Engles, 1,038
Barton Leach, 1,033
Hassan Duncombe, 1,009

MOST CAREER REBOUNDS

Ernie Beck, 1,557
Barton Leach, 1066
Joseph Sturgis, 1,064
Richard Censits, 867
Ron Haigler, 856
Richard Heylmun, 848
Bruce Lefkowitz, 766
Tony Price, 731
Jim Wolf, 684
Corky Calhoun, 682

MOST CAREER ASSISTS

Jerome Allen, 505
Paul Chambers, 396
Matt Maloney, 373
Dave Wohl, 345
Bobby Willis, 317
Mark Lonetto, 299
Karl Racine, 290
Ed Stefanski, 281
James Salters, 258
Walt Frazier, 237

MOST CAREER STEALS

Jerome Allen, 166
Matt Maloney, 157
Paul Chambers, 134
Anthony Arnolie, 117
Barry Pierce, 112

MOST CAREER BLOCKED SHOTS

Tim Krug, 138
Hassan Duncombe, 127
Eric Moore, 66
Shawn Trice, 65
Michael Brown, 51

ALL-TIME COACHING RECORDS

- R.B. Smith, 1905-09, 4 years, 73-22
- Charles Kenath, 1909-12, 3 years, 36-25
- Arthur Kiefaber, 1912-14, 2 years, 10-14
- Lon Jourdet, 1914-43, 19 years, 227-143
- Edward McNichol, 1920-30, 10 years, 186-63
- Donald Kellett, 1943-48, 4 years, 46-31
- Robert Dougherty, 1945-46, 1 year, 7-10
- Howard Dallmar, 1948-54, 6 years, 105-51
- Ray Stanley, 1954-56, 2 years, 31-19
- Jack McCloskey, 1956-66, 10 years, 146-105
- Dick Harter, 1966-71, 6 years, 88-44
- Chuck Daly, 1971-77, 6 years, 125-38
- Bob Weinhauer, 1977-82, 5 years, 99-45
- Craig Littlepage, 1982-85, 3 years, 40-39
- Tom Schneider, 1985-89, 4 years, 51-54
- Fran Dunphy, 1989-96, 7 years, 123-65

PENN'S NATIONAL RANKINGS				
Season	Final AP	AP High	Final AP	UPI High
1969-70	13th	13th	13th	13th
1970-71	Third	Third	Third	Third
1971-72	Second	Second	Third	Third
1972-73	18th	Eighth	20th	Eighth
1973-74	None	11th	None	17th
1974-75	17th	Ninth	11th	11th
1977-78	20th	20th	20th	20th
1978-79	14th	14th	None	None
1993-94	None	24th	—	—
1994-95	—	21st	—	—

ST. JOSEPH RECORDS

ALL-TIME LEADING SCORERS

Bernard Blunt, 1,985
Craig Amos, 1,735
Tony Costner, 1,729
Cliff Anderson, 1,728
Maurice Martin, 1,726
Norman Black, 1,726
Mike Bantom, 1,684
Bob Lojewski, 1,682
Rodney Blake, 1,679
Boo Williams, 1,554
Pat McFarland, 1,545
Dan Kelly, 1,524
Mike Hauer, 1,496
Carlin Warley, 1,480
Paul Senesky, 1,472
Bob McNeill, 1,393
Rap Curry, 1,372
Jack Egan, 1,363
Tom Wynne, 1,321
Bryan Warrick, 1,273
Kurt Engelbert, 1,243
Mark Bass, 1,205
Lonnie McFarlan, 1,152
Reggie Townsend, 1,145
Bill Oakes, 1,129
Tom Duff, 1,103
Bill Lynch, 1,076
Steve Courtin, 1,060
Joe Gallo, 1,053
Wayne Williams, 1,048
Mike Thomas, 1,029
Jim Lynam, 1,012
Zane Major, 1,001

MOST CAREER ASSISTS

Rap Curry, 580
Luke Griffin, 523
Bob McNeill, 442
Maurice Martin, 415
James "Bruiser" Flint, 402
Jim Lynam, 390
Jim O'Brien, 373
Bryan Warrick, 351
Geoff Arnold, 346
Jeffery Clark, 345

MOST CAREER REBOUNDS

Cliff Anderson, 1,228

Mike Bantom, 1,151
Carlin Warley, 1,138
Bill Lynch, 1,107
Mike Hauer, 976
Tony Costner, 951
Norman Black, 906
Kurt Engelbert, 898
Bob Clarke, 877
Jack Egan, 871
Boo Williams, 838
Ray Radziszewski, 834
Rodney Blake, 818
John Connolly, 780
Bernard Blunt, 734
Bob Lojewski, 724
Tom Wynne, 720
Tom Duff, 697
Larry Hoffman, 629
Jim Boyle, 627
Maurice Martin, 622
Mike Thomas, 616
Vince Kempton, 615
Marty Ford, 594
Craig Amos, 588
Greg Mullee, 564
Joe Spratt, 563
Rap Curry, 521
Henry Smith, 518
Kevin Furey, 511
Pat McFarland, 503

MOST CAREER STEALS

Jeffery Clark, 250
Maurice Martin, 248
Luke Griffin, 236
Cliff Anderson, 212
Steve Courtin, 208
Bill DeAngelis, 195
Rap Curry, 195
Bryan Warrick, 181
Mike Moody, 175
Bill Oakes, 168

MOST CAREER BLOCKED SHOTS

Rodney Blake, 419
Tony Costner, 212
Boo Williams, 142
Carlin Warley, 85

Maurice Martin, 75
Ron Vercruyssen, 68
Bob Lojewski, 63
*Zane Major, 55
Norman Black, 50
Kevin Springman, 47
*Total does not include 1975-76 statistics,
which are unavailable in this category.

ALL-AMERICANS

Phil Zuber...1932
Bob McNeill...1960
Matt Guokas, Sr....1938
Matt Guokas, Jr....1966
George Senesky.....1943*
Cliff Anderson.....1967
Kurt Engelburt.....1957
Mike Bantom........1973**
*Helms Foundation
**Member of 1972 U.S. Olympic Team

ALL-TIME COACHING RECORDS

- John Denver, 1909-10, 1 year, 10-6
- Edward Dennis, 1910-11, 1 year, 6-6
- John Donahue, 1911-12 thru 1918-19, 8 years, 78-52
- John Lavin, 1919-20 thru 1925-26, 7 years, 50-62
- Tom Temple, 1926-27 thru 1927-28, 2 years, 12-22
- Bill Ferguson, 1928-29 thru 1954-55, 25 years, 309-208
- John McMenamin, 1953-54 thru 1954-55, 2 years, 26-23,
- Jack Ramsay, 1955-56 thru 1965-66, 11 years, 234-72
- Jack McKinney, 1966-67 thru 1973-74, 8 years, 144-77
- Harry Booth, 1974-75 thru 1977-78, 4 years, 44-61
- Jim Lynam, 1978-79 thru 1980-81, 3 years, 65-28
- Jim Boyle, 1981-82 thru 1989-90, 9 years, 151-114
- John Griffin, 1990-91 thru 1994-95, 5 years, 75-69
- Phil Martelli, 1995-96 thru present, 1 year, 19-13

TEMPLE RECORDS

ALL-TME LEADING SCORERS

Mark Macon, 2,609
Terence Stansbury, 1,811
Guy Rodgers, 1,767
Nate Blackwell, 1,708
Granger Hall, 1,652
Aaron McKie, 1,650
Mike Vreeswyk, 1,650
John Baum, 1,544
Bill Mlkvy, 1,539
Marty Stahurski, 1,499
Rick Brunson, 1,493
Hal Lear, 1,472
Mik Kilgore, 1,471
Eddie Jones, 1,470
Bill Kennedy, 1,468
Howard Evans, 1,459
Bruce Drysdale, 1,444
Tim Claxton, 1,418
Clarence Brookins, 1,386
Tim Perry, 1,368
Jim Williams, 1,306
Ed Coe, 1,177
Charles Rayne, 1,131
Joe Cromer, 1,118
Jim McLoughlin, 1,112
Harry Silcox, 1,111
Keith Parham, 1,092
Walt Montford, 1,067
Ollie Johnson, 1,063
Alton McCullough, 1,051
Rick Reed, 1,031
Jay Norman, 1,024

MOST CAREER REBOUNDS

John Baum, 1,042
Jim Williams, 1,031
Russ Gordon, 995
Tim Perry, 985
Jay Norman, 917

MOST CAREER ASSISTS

Howard Evans, 748
Rick Reed, 564

Nate Blackwell, 533
Rick Brunson, 470
Jim McLoughlin, 389

MOST CAREER BLOCKED SHOTS

Tim Perry, 392
Duane Causwell, 203
Mark Strickland, 177
Eddie Jones, 107
Granger Hall, 77

MOST CAREER STEALS

Mark Macon, 281
Howard Evans, 268
Rick Brunson, 253
Eddie Jones, 197
Aaron McKie, 196

ALL-TIME COACHING RECORDS

- Harry Litwack, 1952-73, 21 years, 373-193
- James Usilton, Sr., 1926-40, 13 years, 205-79
- John Chaney, 1982-present, 14 years, 315-129

- Don Casey, 1973-82, 9 years, 151-94
- Josh Cody, 1942-52, 10 years, 122-104
- Charles Williams, 1894-99, 5 years, 73-32
- Samuel L. Dienes, 1823-26, 3 years, 39-21
- Ernest Messikomer, 1939-42, 3 years, 35-27
- William Nicolai, 1913-17, 4 years, 31-26
- Francois M. D'Eliscu, 1919-23, 4 years, 30-22
- H. Shindle Wingert, 1901-05, 4 years, 20-18
- Frederick Prosch, Jr., 1909-13, 4 years, 17-20
- John T. Rogers, 1899, 1 year, 14-8
- John Crescenzo, 1905-08, 3 years, 14-10
- Elwood Geiges, 1917-18, 1 year, 8-7
- Edward M. McCone, 1908-09, 8-20

TEMPLE MILESTONE VICTORIES

WIN	DATE	OPPONENT	SCORE	COACH
100	1903	Drexel	19-13	H. Shindle Wingert
200	1921	Schuykill	31-29	Francois D'Eliscu
300	12/11/29	Philadelphia Osteopathy	39-31	James Usilton
400	2/22/36	Carnegie Tech	44-32	James Usilton
500	2/20/43	La Salle	47-43	Josh Cody
600	12/22/50	Scranton	75-70	Josh Cody
700	2/21/57	St. John's	80-73	Harry Litwack
800	12/27/62	St. John's	64-51	Harry Litwack
900	12/02/68	Hofstra	93-64	Harry Litwack
1000	1/29/74	Drexel	55-43	Don Casey
1100	2/11/80	Rider	80-64	Don Casey
1200	2/23/85	Massachusetts	50-48	John Chaney
1300	1/12/89	Massachusetts	89-68	John Chaney
1400	1/8/94	George Washington	80-64	John Chaney

VILLANOVA RECORDS

ALL-TIME LEADING SCORERS

Kerry Kittles, 2,243
Keith Herron, 2,170
Bob Schafer, 2,094
Doug West, 2,037
Howard Porter, 2,026
John Pinone, 2,024
Ed Pinckney, 1,865
Larry Hennessy, 1,737
Paul Arizin, 1,684
Alex Bradley, 1,634
Tom Ingelsby, 1,616
Bill Melchionni, 1,612
Hubie White, 1,608
Harold Pressley, 1,572
Johnny Jones, 1,568
Larry Herron, 1,553
Dwayne McLain, 1,544
Tom Greis, 1,504
Lance Miller, 1,468
Chris Ford, 1,433
Wali Jones, 1,428
Kenny Wilson, 1,390
Eric Eberz, 1,397
Greg Woodard, 1,312
Reggie Robinson, 1,309
Stewart Granger, 1,307
Tom Sienkiewicz, 1,271
Jack Devine, 1,263
Hank SiemionTkowski, 1,224
Mark Plansky, 1,217
Rory Sparrow, 1,183
Jim Huggard, 1,184
Harold Jensen, 1,155
Jim Washington, 1,146
Joe Lord, 1,125
John Olive, 1,122
Jimmy Smith, 1,014

MOST CAREER REBOUNDS

Howard Porter, 1,317
Jim Washington, 1,194
Jack Devine, 1,181

Ed Pinckney, 1,107
Harold Pressley, 1,016
Jim Mooney, 1,010
John Pinone, 837
George Raveling, 835
Alex Bradley, 797
Hubie White, 755
Hank Siemiontkowski, 739
Tom Greis, 728
Kerry Kittles, 715
John Olive, 700
Johnny Jones, 694
Lance Miller, 674
Bob Schafer, 638
Mark Plansky, 636
Doug West, 630
Marc Dowdell, 619
Rodney Taylor, 614
Larry Heron, 609
Thomas J. Brennan, 566
Aaron Howard, 562
Reggie Robinson, 559
Keith Herron, 556
Chris Ford, 548
Joe Crews, 544
John Driscoll, 526
Jim O'Brien, 523
Larry Moody, 518

MOST CAREER ASSISTS

Kenny Wilson, 627
Stewart Granger, 595
*Chris Ford, 507
Rory Sparrow, 495
Joe Rogers, 474
Gary McLain, 456
Jonathan Haynes, 446
Alvin Williams, 424
Kerry Kittles, 408
Chris Walker, 404
Whitey Rigsby, 393
Lance Miller, 340
Harold Pressley, 300
Mark Plansky, 291
Dwayne McClain, 287
Tom Ingelsby, 279

Doug West, 257
Tom Sienkiewicz, 251
John Pinone, 233
*Wali Jones, 233
Harold Jensen, 231
Ed Pinckney, 226
Ed Hastings, 219
Marc Dowdell, 207
Steve Lincoln, 200
*Career totals incomplete for the noted players. Assists were an official statistic by the NCAA beginning with the 1970-71 season.

MOST CAREER STEALS

Kerry Kittles, 277
Harold Pressley, 213
Gary Massey, 204
Ed Pinckney, 196
Lance Miller, 190
Chris Walker, 185
Jonathan Haynes, 177
*Stewart Granger, 171
Kenny Wilson, 146
Alvin Williams, 140
Dwayne McClain, 133
Doug West, 127
*John Pinone, 117
Mark Plansky, 112
Gary McLain, 102
*Whitey Rigsby, 101
Harold Jensen, 95
Dwight Wilbur, 91
*Rory Sparrow, 86
*Aaron Howard, 86
*Tom Sienkiewicz, 74
*Career totals incomplete for the noted players. Steals were an officially kept statistic beginning with the 1980-81 season (Rigsby missing 46 games; Sparrow missing 57 games; Howard missing 44 games; Sienkiewicz missing 42 games).

MOST CAREER BLOCKED SHOTS

Tom Greis, 273
Jason Lawson, 270

Ed Pinckney, 253
Jason Lawson, 175
Harold Pressley, 152
Anthony Pelle, 94
Ron Wilson, 66
James Bryson, 59
*Aaron Howard, 51
Doug West, 51
Dwayne McClain, 50
Gary Massey, 46
John Pinone, 38
*Career totals incomplete for the noted players.

ALL-TIME COACHING RECORDS

Michael A. Saxe, 1920-26, six years, 64-30

John J. Cashman, 1926-29, three years, 21-26

George W. Jacobs, 1929-36, seven years, 62-56

Alexander G. Severance, 1936-61, 25 years, 413-201

John J. Kraft, 1961-73, 12 years, 238-95

Roland V. Massimino, 1973-92, 19 years, 357-241

Steve Lappas, 1992-present, four years, 79-46

BIG 5 ALL-TIME RECORDS

BIG 5 ALL-TIME SCORERS

1. Lionel Simmons, La Salle, 3,217
2. Michael Brooks, La Salle, 2,628
3. Mark Macon, Temple, 2,609
4. Kerry Kittles, Villanova, 2,443
5. Keith Herron, Villanova, 2,170
6. Doug West, Villanova, 2,037
7. Howard Porter, Villanova, 2,026
8. John Pinone, Villanova, 2,024
9. Steve Black, La Salle, 2,012
10. Bernard Blunt, St. Joseph's, 1,985
11. Kareem Townes, La Salle, 1,925
12. Ed Pinckney, Villanova, 1,865
13. Terence Stansbury, Temple, 1,811
    Randy Woods, La Salle, 1,811
15. Ralph Lewis, La Salle, 1,807
16. Doug Overton, La Salle, 1,795
17. Guy Rodgers, Temple, 1,767
18. Craig Amos, St. Joseph's, 1,735
19. Tony Costner, St. Joseph's, 1,729
20. Cliff Anderson, St. Joseph's, 1,728
21. Maurice Martin, St. Joseph's, 1,726
    Norman Black, St. Joseph's, 1,726
23. Nate Blackwell, Temple, 1,708
24. Tim Legler, La Salle, 1,699
25. Jack Hurd, La Salle, 1,693
26. Bob Lojewski, St. Joseph's, 1,682
27. Rodney Blake, St. Joseph's, 1,679
    Ken Durrett, La Salle, 1,679
29. Granger Hall, Temple, 1,652

30. Aaron McKie, Temple, 1,650
    Mike Vreeswyk, Temple, 1,650
32. Kevin McDonald, Penn, 1,644
33. Alex Bradley, Villanova, 1,634
34. Tom Ingelsby, Villanova, 1,616
35. Bill Melchionni, Villanova, 1,612
36. Hubie White, Villanova, 1,608
37. Harold Pressley, Villanova, 1,572
38. Johnny Jones, Villanova, 1,568
39. Larry Herron, Villanova, 1,553
40. Billy Taylor, La Salle, 1,554
    Boo Williams, St. Joseph's, 1,554
42. Pat McFarland, St. Joseph's, 1,545
43. John Baum, Temple, 1,544
    Dwayne McClain, Villanova, 1,544
45. Jerome Allen, Penn, 1,518
46. Tom Greis, Villanova, 1,504
47. Stan Pawlak, Penn, 1,501
48. Marty Stahurski, Temple, 1,499
49. Mike Hauer, St. Joseph's, 1,496
50. Rick Brunson, Temple, 1,493
51. Carlin Warley, St. Joseph's, 1,480
52. Hal Lear, Temple, 1,472
53. Mik Kilgore, Temple, 1,471
54. Eddie Jones, Temple, 1,470
55. Bill Kennedy, Temple, 1,468
    Lance Miller, Villanova, 1,468
57. Howard Evans, Temple, 1,459
58. Bruce Drysdale, Temple, 1,444
59. Bruce Lefkowitz, Penn, 1,443
60. Chris Ford, Villanova, 1,433
61. Larry Cannon, La Salle, 1,430
62. Tim Claxton, Temple, 1,418
63. Frank Corace, La Salle, 1,411

64. Eric Eberz, Villanova, 1,397
65. Bob McNeill, St. Joseph's, 1,393
66. Kenny Wilson, Villanova, 1,390
67. Larry Koretz, La Salle, 1,382
68. Bob Morse, Penn, 1,381
69. Rap Curry, St. Joseph's, 1,372
70. Matt Maloney, Penn, 1,370
71. Tim Perry, Temple, 1,368
    Paul Burke, La Salle, 1,368
73. Jack Egan, St. Joseph's, 1,363
74. Kurt Kanaskie, La Salle, 1,356
75. Tony Price, Penn, 1,322
76. Tom Wynne, St. Joseph's, 1,321
77. Greg Woodard, Villanova, 1,312
78. Reggie Robinson, Villanova, 1,309
79. Stewart Granger, Villanova, 1,307
80. Jim Williams, Temple, 1,306
81. Tyrone Pitts, Penn, 1,301
82. Joe Sturgis, Penn, 1,292
83. Bryan Warrick, St. Joseph's, 1,273
84. Tom Sienkiewicz, Villanova, 1,271
85. Perry Bromwell, Penn, 1,265
86. Charlie Wise, La Salle, 1,245
    Barry Pierce, Penn, 1,245
88. Kurt Engelbert, St. Joseph's, 1,243
89. Phil Hankinson, Penn, 1,236
90. Mo Connolly, La Salle, 1,232
91. Bernie Williams, La Salle, 1,230
92. Chip Greenberg, La Salle, 1,227
93. Dave Wohl, Penn, 1,226
94. Richard Censits, Penn, 1,220
95. Mark Plansky, Villanova, 1,217
96. Mark Bass, St. Joseph's, 1,205

97. Jeff Neuman, Penn, 1,187
98. Jim Huggard, Villanova, 1,184
99. Rory Sparrow, Villanova, 1,183
100. Ed Coe, Temple, 1,177
101. Craig Conlin, La Salle, 1,159
102. Harold Jensen, Villanova, 1,155
103. Lonnie McFarlan, St. Joseph's, 1,152
104. Jim Washington, Villanova, 1,146
105. Reggie Townsend, St. Joseph's, 1,145
106. Alonzo Lewis, La Salle, 1,137
107. Charles Rayne, Temple, 1,131
108. Bill Oakes, St. Joseph's, 1,129
109. Donn Wilber, La Salle, 1,127
110. John Olive, Villanova, 1,122
111. Joe Cromer, Temple, 1,118
     Joe Bryant, La Salle, 1,118
113. Paul Little, Penn, 1,116
114. Jim McLoughlin, Temple, 1,112
115. Steve Bilsky, Penn, 1,108
116. Tom Duff, St. Joseph's, 1,103
117. Keith Parham, Temple, 1,092
118. Romaine Haywood, La Salle, 1,083
119. Bill Lynch, St. Joseph's, 1,076
120. Walt Montford, Temple, 1,067
121. Corky Calhoun, Penn, 1,066
122. Ollie Johnson, Temple, 1,063
123. Albert Butts, La Salle, 1,060
124. Steve Courtin, St. Joseph's, 1,060
125. Bob McAteer, La Salle, 1,056
126. Joe Gallo, St. Joseph's, 1,053
127. Alton McCullough, Temple, 1,051
128. Wayne Williams, St. Joseph's, 1,048
129. John Engles, Penn, 1,038
130. Rick Reed, Temple, 1,031

131. Mike Thomas, St. Joseph's, 1,029
132. Jay Norman, Temple, 1,024
133. Bob Fields, La Salle, 1,016
     George Paull, La Salle, 1,016
135. Jimmy Smith, Villanova, 1,014
136. Jim Lynam, St. Joseph's, 1,012
137. Rich Tarr, La Salle, 1,004
138. Zane Major, St. Joseph's, 1,001

BIG 5 ALL-TIME LEADING REBOUNDERS

1. Lionel Simmons, La Salle, 1,429
2. Michael Brooks, La Salle, 1,372
3. Howard Porter, Villanova, 1,317
4. Cliff Anderson, St. Joseph's, 1,228
5. Jim Washington, Villanova, 1,194
6. Mike Bantom, St. Joseph's, 1,151
7. Carlin Warley, St. Joseph's, 1,138
8. Bill Lynch, St. Joseph's, 1,107
9. Ed Pinckney, Villanova, 1,107
10. Joe Sturgis, Penn, 1,064
11. John Baum, Temple, 1,042
12. Jim Williams, Temple, 1,031
13. Russ Gordon, Temple, 995
14. Tim Perry, Temple, 985
15. Mike Hauer, St. Joseph's, 976
16. Ralph Lewis, La Salle, 966
17. Tony Costner, St. Joseph's, 951
18. Jay Norman, Temple, 917
19. Kurt Engelbert, St. Joseph's, 898
20. Bob Clarke, St. Joseph's, 877
21. Jack Egan, St. Joseph's, 871
22. Richard Censits, Penn, 867
23. Ron Haigler, Penn, 856

24. Ken Durrett, La Salle, 850
25. Boo Williams, St. Joseph's, 838
26. John Pinone, Villanova, 837
27. George Raveling, Villanova, 835
28. Ray Radziszewski, St. Joseph's, 834
29. George Sutor, La Salle, 826
30. Rodney Blake, St. Joseph's, 818

BIG 5 ALL-TIME LEADERS IN ASSISTS

1. Howard Evans, Temple, 748
2. Doug Overton, La Salle, 671
3. Kenny Wilson, Villanova, 627
4. Stewart Granger, Villanova, 595
5. Rap Curry, St. Joseph's, 580
6. Paul Burke, La Salle, 567
7. Nate Blackwell, Temple, 533
8. Luke Griffin, St. Joseph's, 523
9. Chris Ford, Villanova, 507
10. Jerome Allen, Penn, 505
11. Rory Sparrow, Villanova, 495
12. Joe Rogers, Villanova, 474
13. Rick Brunson, Temple, 470
14. Darryl Gladden, La Salle, 461
15. Chip Greenberg, La Salle, 461
16. Gary McLain, Villanova, 456
17. Jonathan Haynes, Villanova, 446
18. Bob McNeill, St. Joseph's, 442
19. Rich Tarr, La Salle, 429
20. Maurice Martin, St. Joseph's, 415
21. Charlie Wise, La Salle, 407
22. James "Bruiser" Flint, St. Joseph's, 402
23. Paul Chambers, Penn, 396
24. Whitey Rigsby, Villanova, 393
25. Jim Lynam, St. Joseph's, 390
26. Jim McLoughlin, Temple, 389

ALL BIG 5 TEAMS

The Robert Geasey Award is presented annually by the Temple University Dental Alumni Association to the outstanding Big 5 Player of the Year, by a vote of the Herb Good Basketball Club. Bob Geasey was the former director of public relations at Temple University and managing director of college basketball doubleheaders at Convention Hall.

1955-56
First Team- Dick Censits, Penn; Kurt Engelbert, St. Joseph's; Mike Fallon, St. Joseph's; Al Juliana, St. Joseph's; Hal Lear, Temple; Bill Lynch, St. Joseph's; Fran O'Malley, La Salle; Hal Reinfeld, Temple; Guy Rodgers, Temple; Jimmy Smith, Villanova; Joe Sturgis, Penn
*MVP - Guy Rodgers

1956-57
First Team- Mel Brodsky, Temple; Dick Censits, Penn; Dan Dougherty, St. Joseph's; Kurt Engelburt, St. Joseph's; Tom Garberina, La Salle; Al Griffith, Villanova; Alonzo Lewis, La Salle; Jay Norman, Temple; Ray Radziszewski, St. Joseph's; Guy Rodgers, Temple.
*MVP - Guy Rodgers

1957-58
First Team- Tom Brennan, Villanova; Dick Censits, Penn; Bob McNeill, St. Joseph's; Jay Norman, Temple; Guy Rodgers, Temple.
*MVP - Guy Rodgers

1958-59
First Team- Ralph Bantivoglio, La Salle; Bob Herdelin, La Salle; Bill Kennedy, Temple; Bob McNeill, St. Joseph's; Joe Ryan, Villanova; George Schmidt, Penn; Joe Spratt, St. Joseph's.
*MVP - Joe Spratt

1959-60
First Team- Bob Alden, La Salle; Joe Gallo, St. Joseph's; Jim Huggard, Villanova; Bill Kennedy, Temple; Bob McNeill, St. Joseph's; Bob Mlkvy, Penn; Hubie White, Villanova.
*MVP - Bill Kennedy

1960-61
First Team- Bruce Drysdale, Temple; Jim Huggard, Villanova; Bob McAteer, La Salle; Bob Mlkvy, Penn; Hubie White, Villanova.
*MVP - Bruce Drysdale

1961-62
First Team- Bruce Drysdale, Temple; Wali Jones, Villanova; Bob McAteer, La Salle; Hubie White, Villanova; Tom Wynne, St. Joseph's.
*MVP - Hubie White

1962-63
First Team- Frank Corace, La Salle; Wali Jones, Villanova; Jim Lynam, St. Joseph's; Jim Washington, Villanova; John Wideman, Penn; Tom Wynne, St. Joseph's.
*MVPs - Jim Lynam and Wali Jones

1963-64
First Team- Frank Corace, La Salle; Steve Courtin, St. Joseph's; Wali Jones, Villanova; Jim Washington, Villanova; Jim Williams, Temple.
Honorable Mention- Ray Carazo, Penn; Jeff Neuaman, Penn; Stan Pawlak, Penn; Bob Harrington, Temple.
*MVPs - Wali Jones and Steve Courtin

1964-65

First Team- Cliff Anderson, St. Joseph's; Curt Fromal, La Salle; Matt Guokas, St. Joseph's; Bill Melchionni, Villanova; Jeff Neuman, Penn; Jim Washington, Villanova.
*MVP - Jim Washington

1965-66

First Team- Cliff Anderson, St. Joseph's; Matt Guokas, St. Joseph's; Hubie Marshall, La Salle; Bill Melchionni, Villanova; Jeff Neuman, Penn; Stan Pawlak, Penn; Jim Williams, Temple.
*MVP - Bill Melchionni

1966-67

First Team- Cliff Anderson, St. Joseph's; John Baum, Temple; Clarence Brookins, Temple; Larry Cannon, La Salle; Johnny Jones, Villanova; Hubie Marshall, La Salle.
*MVP - Cliff Anderson

1967-68

First Team- John Baum, Temple; Larry Cannon, La Salle; Mike Hauer, St. Joseph's; Johnny Jones, Villanova; Dan Kelly, St. Joseph's.

Honorable Mention- Pete Andrews, Penn; Bill DeAngelis, St. Joseph's; Bernie Williams, La Salle.
*MVP - Johnny Jones

1968-69

First Team- John Baum, Temple; Larry Cannon, La Salle; Ken Durrett, La Salle; Mike Hauer, St. Joseph's; Johnny Jones, Villanova; Howard Porter, Villanova; Bernie Williams, La Salle.
*MVPs - Howard Porter and Ken Durrett

1969-70

First Team- Corky Calhoun, Penn; Ken Durrett, La Salle; Mike Hauer, St. Joseph's; Dan Kelly, St. Joseph's; Howard Porter, Villanova.
*MVP - Ken Durrett

1970-71

First Team- Corky Calhoun, Penn; Ken Durrett, La Salle; Bobby Fields, La Salle; Bob Morse, Penn; Howard Porter, Villanova.
*MVP - Ken Durrett

1971-72

First Team- Mike Bantom, St. Joseph's; Corky Calhoun, Penn; Chris Ford, Villanova; Phil Hankinson, Penn; Tom Ingelsby, Villanova; Ollie Johnson, Temple; Bob Morse, Penn.
*MVPs - Corky Calhoun and Chris Ford

1972-73

First Team- Mike Bantom, St. Joseph's; Jim Crawford, La Salle; Phil Hankinson, Penn; Tom Ingelsby, Villanova; Pat McFarland, St. Joseph's.
*MVP - Tom Ingelsby

1973-74

First Team- Joe Bryant, La Salle; Ron Haigler, Penn; Mike Moody, St.Joseph's; Jim O'Brien, St. Joseph's; Bill Taylor, La Salle.
*MVP - Ron Haigler

1974-75

First Team- Bob Bigelow, Penn; Joe Bryant, La Salle; Ron Haigler, Penn; Bill Taylor, La Salle; Charlie Wise, La Salle.
*MVP - Ron Haigler

1975-76

First Team- Norman Black, St. Joseph's; John Engles, Penn; Keith Herron, Villanova; Keven McDonald, Penn; Charlie Wise, La Salle.
*MVP - Charlie Wise

1976-77

First Team- Norman Black, St. Joseph's; Michael Brooks, La Salle; Keith Herron, Villanova; Keven McDonald, Penn; Marty Stahurski, Temple.
*MVP - Keven McDonald

1977-78

First Team- Michael Brooks, La Salle; Tim Claxton, Temple; Keith Herron, Villanova; Keven McDonald, Penn; Marty Stahurski, Temple.
*MVP - Michael Brooks

1978-79

First Team- Alex Bradley, Villanova; Michael Brooks, La Salle; Bruce Harrold, Temple; Tony Price, Penn; Rick Reed, Temple; Tim Smith, Penn.
*MVPs - Tony Price and Rick Reed

1979-80

First Team- Alex Bradley, Villanova; Michael Brooks, La Salle; John Pinone, Villanova; James Salters, Penn; Rory Sparrow, Villanova; Boo Williams, St. Joseph's.
*MVP - Michael Brooks

1980-81

First Team- Stewart Granger, Villanova; Kevin Lynam, La Salle; John Pinone, Villanova; Neal Robinson, Temple; Bryan Warwick, St. Joseph's.
*MVP - John Pinone

1981-82

First Team- Steve Black, La Salle; Jeffery Clark, St. Joseph's; Granger Hall, Temple; John Pinone, Villanova; Bryan Warwick, St. Joseph's.

Second Team- Tony Costner, St. Joseph's; Paul Little, Penn; Lonnie McFarlan, St. Joseph's; Ed Pinckney, Villanova; Terence Stansbury, Temple.
*MVPs - John Pinone and Jeffery Clark

1982-83

First Team- Steve Black, La Salle; Bob Lojewski, St. Joseph's; Ed Pinckney, Villanova; John Pinone, Villanova; Terence Stansbury, Temple.

Second Team- Michael Brown, Penn; Tony Costner, St. Joseph's; Stewart Granger, Villanova; Ralph Lewis, La Salle; Paul Little, Penn; Jim McLoughlin, Temple.
*MVPs - John Pinone and Terence Stansbury

1983-84

First Team- Steve Black, La Salle; Granger Hall, Temple; Ralph Lewis, La Salle; Maurice Martin, St. Joseph's; Ed Pinckney, Villanova; Terence Stansbury, Temple.

Second Team- Albert Butts, La Salle; Tony Costner, St. Joseph's; Bob Lojewski, St. Joseph's; Dwayne McClain, Villanova; Jim McLoughlin, Temple.
*MVP - Ralph Lewis

1984-85

First Team- Granger Hall, Temple; Ralph Lewis, La Salle; Maurice Martin, St. Joseph's; Dwayne McClain, Villanova; Ed Pinckney, Villanova.

Second Team- Steve Black, La Salle; Perry Bromwell, Penn; Bob Lojewski, St. Joseph's; Gary McLain, Villanova; Karl Racine, Penn; Charles Rayne, Temple.
*MVP - Ed Pinckney

1985-86

First Team- Rodney Blake, St. Joseph's; Chip Greenberg, La Salle; Maurice Martin, St. Joseph's; Tim Perry, Temple; Harold Pressley, Villanova.

Second Team- Nate Blackwell, Temple; Perry Bromwell, Penn; Ed Coe, Temple; Harold Jensen, Villanova; Wayne Williams, St. Joseph's.
*MVP - Harold Pressley

1986-87

First Team- Nate Blackwell, Temple; Rodney Blake, St. Joseph's; Tim Legler, La Salle; Tim Perry, Temple; Lionel Simmons,

Second Team- Perry Bromwell, Penn; Bruce Lefkowitz, Penn; Harold Jensen, Villanova; Mark Plansky, Villanova; Wayne Williams, St. Joseph's.
*MVP - Nate Blackwell

1987-88

First Team- Rodney Blake, St. Joseph's; Howard Evans, Temple; Mark Macon, Temple; Tim Perry, Temple; Lionel Simmons, La Salle.

Second Team- Tom Greis, Villanova; Tim Legler, La Salle; Mark Plansky, Villanova; Mike Vreeswyk, Temple; Doug West, Villanova.
*MVP - Lionel Simmons

1988-89

First Team- Mark Macon, Temple; Doug Overton, La Salle; Lionel Simmons, La Salle; Mike Vreeswyk, Temple; Chris Walker, Villanova.
*MVP - Lionel Simmons

1989-90

First Team- Donald Hodge, Temple; Mark Macon, Temple; Doug Overton, La Salle; Lionel Simmons, La Salle; Chris Walker, Villanova.

Second Team- Craig Amos, St. Joseph's; Hassan Duncombe, Penn; Tom Gries, Villanova; Jerry Simon, Penn; Randy Woods, La Salle.
*MVP - Lionel Simmons

1990-91

First Team- Bernard Blunt, St. Joseph's; Mark Macon, Temple; Lance Miller, Villanova; Doug Overton, La Salle; Randy Woods, La Salle.

Second Team- Craig Amos, St. Joseph's; Rap Curry, St. Joseph's; Donald Hodge, Temple; Mik Kilgore, Temple; Greg Woodward, Villanova.
*MVP - Mark Macon

1991-92

First Team- Bernard Blunt, St. Joseph's; Jack Hurd, La Salle; Aaron McKie, Temple; Lance Miller, Villanova; Randy Woods, La Salle.

Second Team- Craig Amos, St. Joseph's; Paul Chambers, Penn; Mik Kilgore, Temple; Mark Strickland, Temple.
*MVP - Randy Woods

1992-93

First Team- Jerome Allen, Penn; Bernard Blunt, St. Joseph's; Eddie Jones, Temple; Matt Maloney, Penn; Aaron McKie, Temple.

Second Team- Rick Brunson, Temple; Rap Curry, St. Joseph's; Barry Pierce, Penn; Kareem Townes, La Salle; Carlin Warley, St. Joseph's.
*MVP - Aaron McKie

1993-94

First Team- Jerome Allen, Penn; Eddie Jones, Temple; Kerry Kittles, Villanova; Aaron McKie, Temple; Carlin Warley, St. Joseph's.

Second Team- Rick Brunson, Temple; Rap Curry, St. Joseph's; Matt Maloney, Penn; Barry Pierce, Penn; Kareem Townes, La Salle.
*MVP - Eddie Jones

1994-95

First Team- Jerome Allen, Penn; Rick Brunson, Temple; Kerry Kittles, Villanova; Matt Maloney, Penn; Kareem Townes, La Salle.

Second Team- Paul Burke, La Salle; Eric Eberz, Villanova; Jason Lawson, Villanova; Reggie Townsend, St. Joseph's; Carlin Warley, St Joseph's.
*MVP - Kerry Kittles

1995-96

First Team- Reggie Townsend, St. Joseph's; Jason Lawson, Villanova; Marc Jackson, Temple; Ira Bowman, Penn; Kerry Kittles, Villanova.

Second Team- Alvin Williams, Villanova; Eric Eberz, Villanova; Romaine Haywood, La Salle; Will Johnson, St. Joseph's; Mark Bass, St. Joseph's, Tim Krug, Penn.
*MVP - Kerry Kittles

*denotes The Robert Geasey Memorial Trophy Winner

BIG 5 CITY SERIES PLAY

1955-56
St. Joseph's 4-0
Temple 3-0
La Salle 2-2
Villanova 1-3
Pennsylvania 0-4

1956-57
La Salle 3-1
St. Joseph's 3-1
Temple 3-1
Villanova 1-3
Pennsylvania 0-4

1957-58
Temple 4-0
St. Joseph's 3-1
La Salle 1-3
Pennsylvania 1-3
Villanova 1-3

1958-59
St. Joseph's 4-0
Villanova 3-1
La Salle 1-3
Pennsylvania 1-3
Temple 1-3

1959-60
St. Joseph's 3-1
Villanova 3-1
Pennsylvania 2-2
La Salle 1-3
Temple 1-3

1960-61
St. Joseph's 4-0
Temple 3-1
La Salle 2-2
Pennsylvania 1-3
Villanova 0-4

1961-62
Villanova 4-0
La Salle 2-2
Temple 2-2
Pennsylvania 1-3
St. Joseph's 1-3

1962-63
Pennsylvania 3-1
Villanova 3-1
St. Joseph's 2-2
La Salle 1-3
Temple 1-3

1963-64
La Salle 3-1
St. Joseph's 2-2
Temple 2-2
Villanova 2-2
Pennsylvania 1-3

1964-65
St. Joseph's 4-0
La Salle 2-2
Temple 2-2
Villanova 2-2
Pennsylvania 0-4

1965-66
St. Joseph's 4-0
Temple 3-1
Pennsylvania 2-2
La Salle 1-3
Villanova 0-4

1966-67
Villanova 4-0
Temple 3-1
St. Joseph's 2-2
La Salle 1-3
Pennsylvania 0-4

1967-68
St. Joseph's 3-1
La Salle 2-2
Temple 2-2
Villanova 2-2
Pennsylvania 1-3

1968-69
La Salle 4-0
Villanova 2-2
Temple 2-2
St. Joseph's 1-3
Pennsylvania 1-3

1969-70
Pennsylvania 4-0
Villanova 3-1
St. Joseph's 2-2
Temple 1-3
La Salle 0-4

1970-71
Pennsylvania 4-0
La Salle 2-2
St. Joseph's 2-2
Villanova 2-2
Temple 0-4

1971-72
Pennsylvania 3-1
Temple 3-1
Villanova 2-2
St. Joseph's 2-2
La Salle 0-4

1972-73
Pennsylvania 3-1
St. Joseph's 2-2
Temple 2-2
La Salle 1-3
Villanova 1-3

1973-74
Pennsylvania 4-0
La Salle 2-2
St. Joseph's 2-2
Temple 2-2
Villanova 0-4

1974-75
La Salle 4-0
Pennsylvania 3-1
Villanova 2-2
Temple 1-3
St. Joseph's 0-4

1975-76
St. Joseph's 3-1
Villanova 3-1
Pennsylvania 2-2
La Salle 1-3
Temple 1-3

1976-77
Pennsylvania 3-1
Temple 3-1
Villanova 2-2
La Salle 2-2
St. Joseph's 0-4

1977-78
Temple 3-1
Villanova 3-1
Pennsylvania 2-2
La Salle 2-2
St. Joseph's 0-4

1978-79
Pennsylvania 3-1
Temple 3-1
St. Joseph's 2-2
La Salle 2-2
Villanova 1-3

1979-80
St. Joseph's 4-0
Villanova 3-1
La Salle 1-3
Temple 1-3
Pennsylvania 1-3

1980-81
La Salle 2-2
Pennsylvania 2-2
St. Joseph's 2-2
Temple 2-2
Villanova 2-2

1981-82
St. Joseph's 3-1
Temple 3-1
Villanova 2-2
La Salle 1-3
Pennsylvania 1-3

1982-83
Villanova 3-1
Pennsylvania 2-2
St. Joseph's 2-2
Temple 2-2
La Salle 1-3

1983-84
La Salle 3-1
Temple 3-1
St. Joseph's 2-2
Villanova 2-2
Pennsylvania 0-4

1984-85
Villanova 4-0
La Salle 2-2
St. Joseph's 2-2
Temple 2-2
Pennsylvania 0-4

1985-86
St. Joseph's 3-1
Temple 3-1
Villanova 2-2
La Salle 1-3
Pennsylvania 1-3

1986-87
Temple 4-0
La Salle 2-2
St. Joseph's 2-2
Villanova 2-2
Pennsylvania 0-4

1987-88
Temple 4-0
St. Joseph's 3-1
Villanova 2-2
Pennsylvania 1-3
La Salle 0-4

1988-89
La Salle 3-1
Temple 3-1
Villanova 2-2
Pennsylvania 1-3
St. Joseph's 1-3

1989-90
La Salle 4-0
Villanova 3-1
Temple 2-2
St. Joseph's 1-3
Pennsylvania 0-4

1990-91
St. Joseph's 3-1
Temple 3-1
La Salle 2-2
Villanova 2-2
Pennsylvania 0-4

1991-92
La Salle 1-1
Pennsylvania 1-1
St. Joseph's 1-1
Temple 1-1
Villanova 1-1

1992-93
Temple 2-0
Pennsylvania 1-1
St. Joseph's 1-1
La Salle 1-1
Villanova 0-2

1993-94
Pennsylvania 2-0
Temple 2-0
Villanova 1-1
La Salle 0-2
St. Joseph's 0-2

1994-95
Temple 2-0
St. Joseph's 2-0
Villanova 1-1
Pennsylvania 0-2
La Salle 0-2

1995-96
Temple 2-0
Pennsylvania 1-1
St. Joseph's 1-1
Villanova 1-1
La Salle 0-2

BIG 5 TEAMS IN POSTSEASON PLAY

1955-56

- Temple (NCAA Tournament) defeated Holy Cross, 74-72; Connecticut, 75-69; Canisius, 60-58; lost to Iowa, 83-76; defeated Southern Methodist, 90-81. Finished third place in the tournament.
- St. Joseph's (NIT) defeated Seton Hall, 74-65; lost to Louisville, 89-79; defeated St. Francis of New York, 93-82.

1956-57

- Temple (NIT) defeated Dayton, 77-66; lost to Bradley, 94-66; and defeated St. Bonaventure, 67-50. Finished third place in the tournament.

1957-58

- Temple (NCAA) defeated Maryland, 71-67; Dartmouth, 69-50; lost to Kentucky, 61-60; defeated Kansas State, 67-57. Finished third place in the tournament.
- St. Joseph's (NIT) defeated St. Peter's, 83-72; lost St. Bonaventure, 79-75.

1958-59

- St. Joseph's (NCAA) lost to West Virginia, 95-92, and Navy, 70-56.
- Villanova (NIT) lost to St. John's 75-67.

1959-60

- St. Joseph's (NCAA) lost to Duke, 58-56 and West Virginia, 106-100.
- Villanova (NIT) defeated Detroit, 88-86; lost to Utah, 73-72.
- Temple (NIT) lost to Dayton, 71-52.

1960-61

- St. Joseph's (NCAA) defeated Princeton, 72-67; Wake Forest, 96 86; lost to Ohio State, 95-69; defeated Utah, 127-120 in four overtime. Finished third place in the tournament.
- Temple (NIT) lost Dayton, 62-60.

1961-62

- Villanova (NCAA) defeated West Virginia, 90-75; New York University, 79-76; lost to Wake Forest, 76-69.
- St. Joseph's (NCAA) lost Wake Forest, 96-85 and New York University, 94-85. Temple (NIT) Temple defeated Providence, 80-78; lost to Loyola/Illinois, 75-64.

1962-63

- St. Joseph's (NCAA) defeated Princeton, 82-81; defeated West Virginia, 97-88; lost to Duke, 73-59. Villanova (NIT) defeated DePaul, 63-51; Wichita, 54-53; lost to Canisius, 61-46 and Marquette, 66-58. Finished fourth place in the tournament.
- La Salle (NIT) lost to St. Louis, 62-61.

1963-64

- Villanova (NCAA) defeated Providence, 77-66; lost to Duke, 87-73; defeated Princeton, 74-62.
- Temple (NCAA) lost to Connecticut, 53-48.
- St. Joseph's (NIT) defeated Miami of Florida, 86-76, and lost to Bradley, 83-81.

1964-65

- St. Joseph's (NCAA) defeated Connecticut, 67-61; lost to Providence, 81-73; lost to North Carolina, 103-81.
- Villanova (NIT) defeated Manhattan, 73-71; New York University, 91-69; and lost to St. John's, 55-51. Finished second place in the tournament.
- La Salle (NIT) lost to Detroit, 93-86.

1965-66

- St. Joseph's (NCAA) defeated Providence, 65-48; lost to Duke, 76-74; defeated Davidson, 92-76. Villanova (NIT) defeated St. John's, 63-61; Boston College, 86-85; lost New York University, 69-63; defeated Army, 76-65. Finished third place in the tournament.
- Temple (NIT) beat Virginia Tech, 88-73 and lost to Kansas, 82-76.

1966-67

- Temple (NCAA) lost to St. John's, 57-53.
- Villanova (NIT) lost to Marshall, 70-69.

1967-68

- La Salle (NCAA) lost Columbia, 83-69.
- Villanova (NIT) defeated Wyoming, 77-66; lost to Kansas, 55-49.
- Temple (NIT) lost to Kansas, 82-76.

1968-69

- Villanova (NCAA) lost to Davidson, 75-61.

- St. Joseph's (NCAA) lost to Duquesne, 74-52.
- Temple (NIT) defeated Florida, 82-66; St. Peter's, 94-78; Tennessee, 63-58; Boston College, 89-76. NIT Champions.

1969-70
- Villanova (NCAA) defeated Temple, 77-69; defeated Niagara, 98-73; lost to St. Bonaventure, 94-74.
- Penn (NCAA) lost to Niagara, 79-69.
- Temple lost to Villanova, 77-69.

1970-71
- Villanova (NCAA) defeated St. Joseph's (93-75); defeated Fordham, 85-75; defeated Pennsylvania, 90-47; defeated Western Kentucky, 92-89 and lost to UCLA, 68-62. Finished second in the tournament.
- St. Joseph's (NCAA) lost to Villanova, 93-75.
- Penn (NCAA) defeated Duquesne, 70-65, defeated South Carolina,79-64; lost Villanova, 90-47.
- La Salle (NIT) lost to Georgia Tech, 70-67.

1971-72
- Penn (NCAA) defeated Providence, 76-60; defeated Villanova, 78-67; lost to North Carolina, 73-59.
- Villanova (NCAA) defeated East Carolina, 85-70; lost to Penn, 78-67; lost to South Carolina, 90-78.
- Temple (NCAA) lost to South Carolina, 53-51.
- St. Joseph's (NIT) lost to Maryland, 67-55.

1972-73
- Penn (NCAA) defeated St. John's, 62-61; lost to Providence, 87-65 and lost to Syracuse, 69-68.
- St. Joseph's (NCAA) lost to Providence, 89-76.

1973-74
- Penn (NCAA) lost to Providence, 84-69.
- St. Joseph's (NCAA) lost to Pitt, 54-42.

1974-75
- Penn (NCAA) lost to Kansas, 69-62.
- La Salle (NCAA) lost to Syracuse, 87-73.

1975-76
No Big 5 teams participated in postseason play.

1976-77
- Villanova (NIT) defeated Old Dominion, 71-68; defeated Massachusetts, 81-71; lost to St. Bonaventure, 86-82; defeated Alabama, 102-89. Finished third place in the tournament.

1977-78
- Villanova (NCAA) defeated La Salle, 103-97; defeated Indiana, 61-60; lost to Duke, 80-72.
- Penn (NCAA) defeated St. Bonaventure, 92-83; lost to Duke, 84-80.
- La Salle (NCAA) lost to Villanova, 103-97.
- Temple (NIT) lost to Texas, 72-58.

1978-79
- Penn (NCAA) defeated Iona, 73-69; defeated North Carolina, 72-71; defeated Syracuse, 84-76; defeated St. John's, 64-62; lost to Michigan State, 101-67; lost to DePaul, 96-93. Penn finished fourth place in the tournament.
- Temple (NCAA) lost to St. John's, 75-70.
- St. Joseph's (NIT) lost to Ohio State, 80-66.

1979-80
- Villanova (NCAA) defeated Marquette, 77-59; lost to Syracuse, 97-83.

- Penn (NCAA) defeated Washington State, 62-55; lost to Duke, 52-42.
- La Salle (NCAA) lost to Purdue, 90-82.
- St. Joseph's (NIT) lost to Texas, 70-61.

1980-81
- St. Joseph's (NCAA) defeated Creighton, 59-57; defeated DePaul, 49-48; defeated Boston College, 42-41; lost to Indiana, 78-46.
- Villanova (NCAA) defeated Houston, 90-72; lost to Virginia, 54-50.
- Temple (NIT) defeated Clemson, 90-82; lost to West Virginia, 77-76. OT.

1981-82
- Villanova (NCAA) defeated 76-72 in triple overtime; defeated Memphis State, 70-66 in overtime; lost to North Carolina, 70-66.
- St. Joseph's (NCAA) lost to Northeastern, 63-62.
- Penn lost to St. John's, 66-56.
- Temple (NIT) lost to Georgia, 73-60.

1982-83
- Villanova (NCAA) defeated Lamar, 60-58; defeated Iowa, 55-54; lost to Houston, 89-71.
- La Salle defeated Boston University, 70-58; lost to Virginia Commonwealth, 76-67.

1983-84
- Temple (NCAA) defeated St. John's, 65-63; lost to North Carolina, 77-66.
- Villanova (NCAA) defeated Marshall, 84-72; lost to Illinois, 64-56.
- La Salle (NIT) lost to Pittsburgh, 75-71.
- St. Joseph's (NIT) lost to Boston College, 76-63.

1984-85

- Villanova (NCAA) defeated Dayton, 51-49; defeated Michigan, 59-55; defeated Maryland, 46-43; defeated North Carolina, 56-44; defeated Memphis State, 52-45; defeated Gerogetown, 66-64. National Champions.
- Temple (NCAA) defeated Virginia Tech, 60-57; lost to Georgetown, 63-46.
- Penn (NCAA) lost to Memphis State, 67-55.
- St. Joseph's (NIT) defeated Missouri, 68-67; lost to Virginia, 68-61.

1985-86

- St. Joseph's (NCAA) defeated Richmond, 60-59; lost to Cleveland State, 75-59.
- Temple (NCAA) defeated Jacksonville, 61-50 in overtime; lost to Kansas, 65-43.
- Villanova (NCAA) defeated Virginia Tech, 71-62; lost to Georgia Tech, 66-61.

1986-87

- Temple (NCAA) defeated Southern, 75-56; lost to LSU, 72-62.
- Penn (NCAA) lost to North Carolina, 113-82.
- La Salle (NIT) defeated Villanova, 86-84; defeated Niagara, 89-81; defeated Illinois State, 70-50; defeated Arkansas Little Rock, 92-73; lost to Southern Mississippi, 94-80. NIT Runnerup.
- Villanova (NIT) lost to La Salle, 86-84.

1987-88

- Temple (NCAA) defeated Lehigh, 87-73; defeated Georgetown, 74-53; defeated Richmond, 69-47; lost to Duke, 63-53.
- Villanova (NCAA) defeated Arkansas, 82-74; Illinois, 66-63; defeated Kentucky, 80-74; lost to Oklahoma, 78-59.
- La Salle (NCAA) lost to Kansas State, 66-53.

1988-89

- La Salle (NCAA) lost to Louisiana Tech, 83-74.
- Villanova (NIT) defeated St. Peter's, 76-56; defeated Penn State, 76-67; lost to Michigan State, 70-63.
- Temple (NIT) lost to Richmond, 70-56.

1989-90

- La Salle (NCAA) defeated Southern Mississippi, 79-63; lost to Clemson, 79-75.
- Temple lost to St. John's, 81-65.
- Villanova (NCAA) lost to LSU, 70-63.

1990 - 91

- Temple (NCAA) defeated Purdue, 80-63; defeated Richmond, 77-64; defeated Oklahoma State, 72-63 in overtime; lost to North Carolina, 75-72.
- Villanova (NCAA) defeated Princeton, 50-48; lost to North Carolina, 84-69.
- La Salle (NIT) lost to Massachusetts, 93-90.

1991-92

- Temple (NCAA) lost to Michigan, 73-66.

- La Salle (NCAA) lost to Seton Hall, 78-76.
- Villanova (NCAA) lost to Virginia, 83-80.

1992-93

- Temple (NCAA) defeated Missouri, 75-61; defeated Santa Clara, 68-57; defeated Vanderbilt, 67-59; lost to Michigan, 77-72.
- Penn (NCAA) lost to Massachusetts, 54-50.
- St. Joseph's (NIT) lost to Southwest Missouri State, 56-34.

1993-94

- Penn (NCAA) defeated Nebraska, 90-80; lost to Florida, 70-58.
- Temple (NCAA) defeated Drexel, 61-39; lost to Indiana, 67-58.
- Villanova (NIT) defeated Canisius, 103-79, defeated Duquesne, 82-66; defeated Xavier, 76-74; defeated Siena, 66-58; defeated Vanderbilt, 80-73. National Champions.

1994-95

- Penn (NCAA) lost to Alabama, 91-85 in overtime.
- Temple (NCAA) lost to Cincinnati, 77-71
- Villanova (NCAA) lost to Old Dominion, 89-81 in three overtimes.
- St. Joseph's (NIT) lost to Coppin State, 75-68 in overtime.

1995-96

- Temple (NCAA) defeated Oklahoma, 61-43, lost to Cincinnati, 78-68
- Villanova (NCAA) defeated Portland, 92-58; lost to Louisville, 68-64.
- St. Joseph's (NIT)